INTERNAL SECURITY

INTERNAL SECURITY

Prof. Emeritus S. Narayan

KALPAZ

First Published, 2018

Published by

Kalpaz Publications
C-30, Satyawati Nagar,
Delhi – 110052
Ph.: 011-47034999, 9811692060
www.kalpazpublications.com
E-mail: kalpaz@hotmail.com

Printed at: G. Print Process, Delhi

Cataloging in Publication Data—DK
Courtesy: D.K. Agencies (P) Ltd. <docinfo@dkagencies.com>

Narayan, S. (Sachindra), 1947- **author.**
Internal security / by S. Narayan.
pages cm
ISBN 9789353240042

1. Internal security. 2. Peace-building. I. Title.

LCC HV6419.N37 2018 | DDC 363.32 23

Contents

Preface

Internal Security is very facinating subject. It attracted my attention in 1966 when we were in a remote tribal village .Teacher who was with us wanted to dug out and take along us a stone statue of Lord Hanumanji, tribals came to know and surrounded us, it was night, police station was far off, no mode of communication. Revenue clerk of the area was living in the village, he went to police station on his bicycle it took 8 hours and we were freed by the tribal when adequate money was to perform rituals to appease village deity which got angered because village deity was dugged out, had the police not come? I do not know what would have been our fate.

This is a very small incident but amply demonstrate the role of Internal Security in our life. No society, No country can run without a proper internal security.

Internal Security is largely perceived as an agency, a Ministry responsible for upholding integrity and sovereignity of the country and maintaining peace in the society and thereby globally. Each country attach due importance to Internal Security. They have ministry for it and similarly each state of the country also have similar department to run the state.

This is not a new subject we find reference of Internal Security in our scriptures, mythology, folklore, folk tales, etc. Today we are in space age and of cyber crime age hence Format and Nature of Internal Security deserve special consideration. Internal security needs to be considered as a tool of world peace. World is now considered as global villages as each country is having similar perspective and dynamics on the subject

Creativity is an important factor of Internal Security which is missing currently from the subject. We ought to have uniform creativity input globally in the retest of global internal security. Further we also need to have uniformity in policy of Internal Security of each country in the interest of the people of globe.

This book will give you insight on the subject. Your suggestions are most welcome to incorporate. In subsequent edition, I am thankful to my wife Mrs Shobha Narayan and our children Dr Shiwani, Prakash Chutru, Dr Savidhi Ajeet, Miss Bhamini, Mr Subhash, master Prakhar and all family members.

I am sincerely thankful to Mr Amit Garg and his father Mr Garg who published the book well in time. One thing I would like to mention here that Mr Garg published my first book Social Anthropology in 1980 and now his son Mr Amit is publishing my 43rd book and more so they not only publish book but maintains family relationship also.

Professor Emeritus S. Narayan
Member

Commission on Nomadic Tribes
govt. of India and formerly in NHRC
former director A N Sinha Institute, Patna
former SK Dey chair Professor, former scientist of ISRO
and formerly Member Task Force on Panchyat govt. of Bihar,
RUSA govt. of Jharkhand Etc.

Chapter - 1

Introduction

Internal security, or IS, is the act of keeping peace within the borders of a sovereign state or other self-governing territories. generally by upholding the national law and defending against internal security threats. Responsibility for internal security may range from police to paramilitary forces, and in exceptional circumstances, the military itself.

Governmental responsibility for internal security will generally rest with an interior ministry, as opposed to a defence ministry. Depending on the state, a state's internal security will be maintained by either the ordinary police or law enforcement agencies or more militarised police forces (known as Gendarmerie or, literally, the Internal Troops.). Other specialised internal security agencies may exist to augment these main forces, such as border guards, special police units, or aspects of the state's intelligence agencies. In some states, internal security may be the primary responsibility of a secret police force.

The level of authorised force used by agencies and forces responsible for maintaining internal security might range from unarmed police to fully armed paramilitary organisations, or employ some level of less-lethal weaponry in between. For violent situations, internal security forces may contain some element of military type equipment such as non-military armored vehicles.

Threats to the general peace may range from low-level civil disorder, large scale violence, or even an armed insurgency. Threats to internal security may be directed at either the state's citizens, or the organs and infrastructure of the state itself, and may range from petty crime, serious organised crime, political or industrial unrest, or even domestic terrorism. Foreign powers may also act as a threat to internal security, by either committing or sponsoring terrorism or rebellion, without actually declaring war.

Governmental responsibility for internal security will generally rest with an interior ministry, as opposed to a defence ministry. Depending on the state, a state's internal security will be maintained by either the ordinary police or law enforcement agencies or more militarised police forces (known as Gendarmerie or, literally, the Internal Troops.). Other specialised internal security agencies may exist to augment these main forces, such as border guards, special police units, or aspects of the state's intelligence agencies. In some states, internal security may be the primary responsibility of a secret police force.

The level of authorised force used by agencies and forces responsible for maintaining internal security might range from unarmed police to fully armed paramilitary organisations, or employ some level of less-lethal weaponry in between. For violent situations, internal security forces may contain some element of military type equipment such as non-military armored vehicles.

Chapter - 2

Internal Security of India

Since the advent of independence, India has faced multitude of security challenges to its nationhood - both external and internal - and to its emergence as a deservingly significant player in the global order. Located in one of the most security and politically stressed regions of the world, and with some not so friendly neighbours, sharing nearly 7000 km of active international borders with seven nations, and a coastline spanning over 15000 km, India's external security challenges are indeed formidable.

External challenges, in today's increasingly troubled world, are by no means, exclusive in their orientation and impact. India's internal security challenges, since decades, have also been pronouncedly sponsored and largely influenced by external machinations and subterfuge. However, it is also an accepted reality that, in recent times, external and internal threats do overlap seamlessly, apart from having multiplied in their intensity. Asymmetric and proxy wars are part of this new dynamic.

Over the last 70 years, India's internal conflicts have ranged from Pakistani planned and supported insurgency, terrorism in Jammu and Kashmir and other Indian states, on-off-on internal unrest in some of India's restive North-Eastern (NE) states including Assam. Additionally, persistent efforts by Pakistan's notorious spy agency, the Inter Services Intelligence (ISI), to foment communal trouble in Punjab and fan 'Khalistani' separatism, growing Naxal-Maoist Left Wing Extremism (LWE) threats in India's hinterland, occasional sectarian, communal and language tensions, organised crime, money laundering, drug trafficking and now cyber driven crimes are the major internal security challenges confronting the Indian state. That since the last 2 years or so there has also been an upsurge in undesirable right wing extremist tendencies among some fringe elements inside India cannot be denied.

Common Factors Impacting Internal Security in India

Internal Security has many constituents and apart from external influences impacting it, there exist certain common factors which , historically, impinged its contours in the Indian context. Some of these are briefly discussed below.

India is home to countless faiths and sub faiths, cultures, castes, languages, regions, customs and its diversity, though uniquely beautiful, is indeed mind boggling. By conservative estimates, India is home to nearly 1660 languages (22 official) and dialects, nearly 3000 castes and sub-castes and virtually all known world religions - making India, indeed, a microcosm of the world. Unquestionably, India's quintessential strength lies in this diversity, yet it also lends itself to major internal strife when provoked both from within or by external influences. The other nation born from the womb of Mother India since the parent nation's violent partition in 1947, Pakistan, remains obsessively anti-India, grossly interfering in India's internal affairs, fanning terrorism not only in Jammu and Kashmir (J and K) but in some other states also besides endeavouring to foist separatist feelings in some states of India, notably Punjab, Assam and in Naxal-Maoist afflicted regions. Pakistan's continuing mischief inside India has adversely afflicted India's internal security health - a factor which successive Indian governments have tended to underestimate despite wars with Pakistan in 1947-48, 1965, 1971 and the 1999 Kargil conflict.

Mediocre and insensitive governance in some states, especially those reeking in poverty and caste divides, also lend themselves to adverse internal conflicts within the nation. One of the major reasons leading to the alarming growth of LWE can be clearly attributed to this factor plaguing the nation apart from other aspects which lend themselves to the growth in LWE. Some politicians of varying ideological hues, pandering to their local vote banks indulge in electoral communal mobilisation by provoking imaginary divides, and stoke the fires of regionalism and separatism for temporary gains. That the people of India, through whom an invisible but an eternal strand symbolizing "Unity in Diversity" runs, have thwarted such devious ambitions of some politicians, time and again, is the saving grace.

India is now a youth- predominant nation, with over 65 percent of its population being under 35 years, which makes India into a very aspirational society. Millions of youth seek suitable employment, better living standards and a million dreams of theirs remain to be fulfilled. Any delays on such vital societal issues automatically contributes to economic and social frustrations which may lead to serious law and order problems besides youth finding their way to anti-national organisations including being influenced by international terror, smuggling networks *et al.* The nuances of some of the serious internal security challenges and suggested national response to contain/manage/eliminate the internal conflicts within India are discussed briefly in the succeeding paragraphs.

Tackling Terrorism and Asymmetric Warfare

Since the last many decades, the phenomenon of terrorism has been an alarmingly spreading scourge of the modern age. One of the nations most affected by it has been India owing to its neighbour, Pakistan, having adopted terrorism as an extension of state policy to destabilize India. Not only in J and K but in other Indian states too, Pakistan has been zealously pursuing its anti-India, though myopic policies, of fomenting terror and unrest. As universally accepted after the 9/11 terror attacks in the US homeland, Pakistan is the fountainhead of most terror activities all over the world. However, now Pakistan is also suffering from intense terror activity perpetrated by those very 'terror tanzeems' it had raised to carry out its devious missions in neighbouring India and Afghanistan. Regrettably, Pakistan so far refuses to see reason with radicalism even permeating its official establishment while its sane civil society dwindles rapidly. Being a nuclear armed "failing state" and coupled with rise in extremism makes Pakistan portend grave dangers for India. As we cannot expect to witness any major changes in Pakistan's highly anti-India policies, it is crucially imperative for the Indian security establishment to factor in all security and terror scenarios which may afflict India from its perpetually belligerent western neighbour, now being substantially supported by its mentor, China. That Pakistan is a proxy for China, against India, brooks no explanation.

India's security establishment will also now have to be alive to threats emanating from global Islamic jihadi outfits like Al Qaida, the Taliban in the Af-Pak region and now, alarmingly also from Daesh (Islamic State, or IS). Though Indian Muslim youth have remained unaffected from their vile propagandas, yet a few appear to have been affected within the nation and thus monitoring the movement of Muslim youth to the Middle East will have to be ensured. Intelligence agencies will have to keep under surveillance social media channels which try to influence/ recruit Muslim youth for terrorist activities as exemplified by ISIS websites. That these global jihadi outfits will collaborate their activities in the Indian sub-continent with Pakistani based so-called non-state actors like the Lashkar-e-Taiyabba, Jaish-e-Mohd, Hizb-ul-Mujaihdeen among many other terror 'tanzeems' in Pakistan, remains a distinct and dangerous possibility. As the security organs of the nation further streamline their functioning by synergetic endeavour and undertake better counter-terror capacity building, the central government has to speedily undertake additional measures to further strengthen our counter-terror and response mechanisms. All political parties in India must not politicize terror and a broad national consensus among all these parties must be reached on the national strategy and measures to be adopted to combat terror.

Secondly, in keeping with the nation's resolve, India must prepare hard-hitting pre-emptive strike plans on terrorist infrastructure in POK and elsewhere in Pakistan, as and when required. Thirdly, India must determinedly endeavour to constantly improve its intelligence gathering, analysis and dissemination machinery - both HUMINT and TECHINT. Pakistan has to be made to realize, both through dialogue and, failing which, by speedy and effective kinetic responses, that terrorism against India will not pay. Stern action against all indigenous separatist leaders must be taken in case they continue to indulge in anti-national or any form of secessionist activities. India must never be seen as a soft state, either by nations inimical to us and, importantly, by its own citizens. Importantly, India has to raise the costs for Pakistan whenever it indulges in mischief. Additionally, Pakistan has to be reminded that till date, India has not exploited Pakistan's many fault-lines and India's strategic restraint is not India's permanent policy.

It is unfortunate that even though we have a strong government at the Centre, the internal security situation of the country has not shown any marked improvement over what it inherited from the UPA regime. This has essentially been because the fundamentals of security management have not been given due importance and, like previous governments, the NDA regime has also preferred to swim with the tide in areas where bold departures were called for.

Successive governments have not cared to codify the country's internal security doctrine and the present government has also ignored this vital area and taken ad hoc decisions on crucial matters. The US and UK revise their national security doctrines every year and place them in the public domain. We have done nothing of the sort, despite the fact that our internal security problems are far more complex. There is no long-term policy for Jammu and Kashmir, nor is there any strategic vision to tackle the Maoist insurgency. No wonder, while violence levels are periodically brought down, they spiral again, and it becomes a game of snakes and ladders.

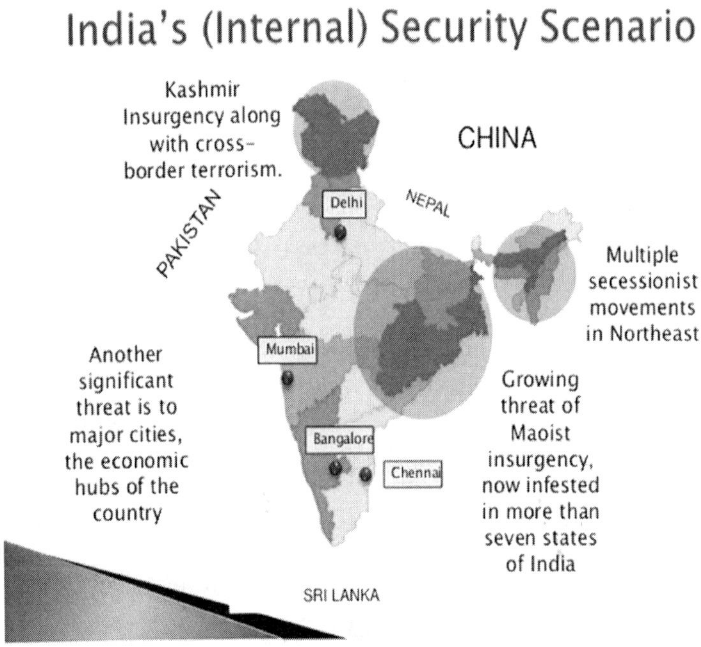

India's Internal Security Threats and Origin

India possesses Internal Security threats from various sources and the reasons for it are very complex to comprehend. However, a lucid understanding of all the factors is important form the point of view of UPSC and other exams. So, below is a list of factors creating Internal Security compulsions for India

a. **Mutual Distrust among South Asian Nations:** The consolidation of South Asian nations into their new identities had resulted into mutual distrust in their relations. Tensions between pluralist democratic governments and unitary form of non-pluralist governments in the sub-continent further add to the imbalances and tensions.

b. **Trans-border impact of Social Tensions:** South Asia consists of numerous ethnic, religious and linguistic groups which often indulge in violent clashes among themselves. Such violence is transnational in nature and impacts the internal security situation across the border. Traditional linkages of friendship and interaction amongst people have become competing arrangements for aiding and abetting subversion, terrorism and insurgencies.

c. **Peculiar position with respect to drugs trade:** Two of the three major narcotic centres of the world, the Golden Crescent in the North-West and the Golden Triangle in the East have made India vulnerable to drug trafficking.

d. **Diverse Socio-Political Milieu of India:** The domestic dynamic of India's Internal Security is reflected in its socio-political milieu consisting of variety of communities, castes, ethnicities, religion, languages, customs and traditions, all operating in a dynamic environment.

e. **Failure to integrate diverse sections of Indian society:**Indian democratic state has had various failures in welding the various sections of society together. This has created conflict situation to the point of violence; and issues of ethno-nationalism and identity are an outcome of this failure only.

f. **Vote Bank Politics to manipulate emotional sensitivities:**Various political parties have manipulated the emotional sensitivities of different communities in order to gain their vote bank. This has created communal tensions and led to radicalisation of individuals.

g. **Uneven economic development and unfulfilled aspirations of the people:** The unjust distribution of economic development and development benefits has driven affected groups to assert themselves and the main target is government, both local and central.

h. **Trans-Border Migration from Bangladesh:** It is a major factor for the problems in Assam and other areas of the North-East. Their transgression into land matters and provision of cheap labour by them is a cause of social and economic insecurity for local communities and a cause of tension and violence.

i. **Politicisation of all problems:** Indian political space has sort of lost its ideological and moral moorings. As a result of politicisation and aggravation of all problems, democratic freedom and electoral politics have led to agitation and unrest. More than any other single factor, the exploitation of diversities has resulted in breakdown of the cohesiveness of the society, created insecurity of cultural identity, encouraged religious revivalism in its fundamentalist form, heightened ethnicity and widened the gap between the sub-national groups and nationalism.

j. **Information Technology (IT) War:** The modern day IT has revolutionised warfare and provided means to the underworld to expand their reach for criminal activities without direct physical involvement.

k. **The China Factor to Internal Security:** The Chinese are believed to have resorted to giving financial aid, arms and sanctuaries to Naga, Mizo and Meitei extremists in the North Eastern states. China is also trying for a strategic containment of India by forming regional alliances and arming India's neighbours Myanmar, Bangladesh and Pakistan.

l. **The Pakistan Factor to Internal Security:** Over the years, Pakistan has supported state sponsored terrorism to create unrest in India. Pakistan has established bases in Nepal, Bangladesh, Sri Lanka and the Middle East- the plan aims at encirclement of India. This combined with the upsurge in Islamic Terrorism at the global level with its epicentre in Central Asian Republic, Afghanistan and Pakistan is likely to have persistent affect on India's internal security.

m. **Jammu and Kashmir Conflict:** The conflict in Jammu and Kashmir has provided ingression to foreign extremist in the country. The people in the state and the minority community at large have been alienated by the Indian state due to the violent and less developed situation in J and K.

n. **Insurgencies in North-East:** North-East is an extremely heterogeneous region with high level of ethnic, cultural, linguistic and religious diversity. The region has witnessed violence due to various reasons ranging from secession to autonomy, movements against foreigners and immigrants, ethnic integration and looking back to their roots as a reaction to perceived imposition of Indianness.

o. **Punjab Terrorism:** Punjab terrorism was the outcome of political ineptness and drew its strength and legitimacy not from any ideology or religious sanction but from the failures of political institutions, governance and administration. It, along with increased narcotic trade, still has the capacity to subvert the peace of the region.

p. **Left Wing Extremism:** The uneven development pattern coupled with rising poverty and unemployment had prevailed in the interior regions of the country. This has created a very dangerous situation of Maoism/ Naxalism/ Left Wing Extremism. In 2006, the then PM even regarded it as the biggest security threat to the nation.

Chapter - 3

Internal Security of Burma

Human security has become a popular political cause, but for, Burma, the state uses national security to subvert human security leaving this up to the international community. National security issues have often served as a smokescreen for oppression in countries like Burma, but now there is a growing recognition that real security must serve people, not enslave them. In September, Thai Foreign Minister Surin Pitsuwan called on the international community to put human security and people-centred development at the heart of foreign policy. Surin, Thailand's talented chief diplomat, stressed: "One cannot have support for human security and effectively pursue people-centered development if one is unable to ensure that people are protected from abuse, suffering and deprivation." Indeed, human security is an issue of the 21st century and it should not be treated lightly. Over the past few years, as the security of states has increased, the security of citizens around the world has declined. An increase in armed conflicts, civil wars, terrorism and large-scale atrocities and genocide are warning signs that the security of ordinary people is at stake. Casualties from armed conflict have doubled over the past decade, with approximately one million people losing their lives each year. Moreover, environmental deterioration, drug trafficking, internally displaced persons, refugee exodus and diseases present further threats to the well being of world citizens. Thailand's foreign minister is himself well aware of what is really happening in his neighbouring country, Burma, where the safety and security of ordinary Burmese have been threatened for decades. The aggressive government in Burma has been threatening the security, safety and well being of Burmese citizens for over a decade. The military leaders have repeatedly used "security" to justify oppression against their own people.

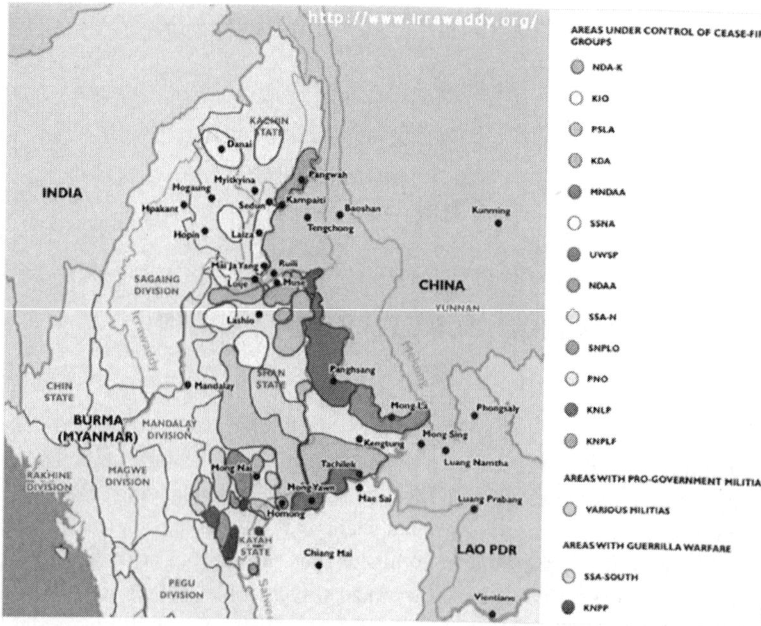

Every time the international community condemns them for their human rights abuses, the leaders invoke "security" as an excuse to justify their crimes. For instance, Nobel Peace Prize laureate Aung San Suu Kyi was recently stopped from travelling outside the capital for "security reasons." Meanwhile, a group of young students has been thrown into prison for years because they posed "a threat to national security." In an address in Ottawa in 1999, Canadian Foreign Minister Lloyd Axworthy stated, "Human security does not supplant national security.

A human security perspective asserts that the security of the state is not an end in itself. Rather, it is a means of ensuring security for its people." Burma is a case study of how people may be deprived of their human security by a handful of military rulers acting in the name of national security. The Burmese people have become victims of the generals' notion of security, rather than its beneficiaries. People may be rounded up simply for listening to short-wave radio stations or talking to foreigners. "Preventive measures" are also taken by the military forces: opposition leaders are put in prison or under house arrest for the sake of "security." It hardly needs to be asked for whose security these measures are really being taken. On other levels as well, the security of the Burmese people has been severely compromised by military rule. According to a World Bank report released last year, social and economic misery in Burma have deepened greatly at the hands of the country's despotic rulers. And international authorities on the HIV/Aids crisis have warned repeatedly that the generals' attitude of denial could doom an entire generation of Burmese in the not too distant future. Meanwhile, Burma has been identified as "one of the real black spots around the world in terms of anti-personnel landmines" by Stephen Goose, founder of the International Campaign to Ban Landmines adding yet another item to Burma's list of "world's worst" standings. UN special investigator Rajsoomer Lallah has more appalling stories. In his latest annual report, the special investigator cited reports of massacres in which more than 100 minority people had been killed since the beginning of this year. His report indicated that some of the worst violence by the military has been committed against ethnic minorities, particularly the Shan, Karen, Karenni and Rohingya groups. Clearly, for this very sizeable segment of Burma's population, there is little comfort to be taken in the regime's claims that it has brought unprecedented peace and security to the country. Plan of Action The question now is how to end or prevent such humanitarian crises and state terrorism. So far, there is no clear answer. The outgoing Canadian foreign minister has proposed at the United Nations the creation of an international commission on intervention and state sovereignty.

Burma's national security and defence posture

Challenges to Burma's security posed by armed separatist and communist insurgencies since independence in 1948 are examined in relation to the responses and initiatives taken by the tatmadaw (Burmese armed forces). It seems that threat perceptions in the context of such challenges and Burma's strict neutrality in international relations, together with budgetary constraints, have shaped the national defence posture. This is reflected in the objectives, means and resources of the tatmadaw which is overwhelmingly oriented towards internal security concerns.

World report 2018: Burma

Burma's stalled democratic transition gave way to a massive human rights and humanitarian crisis starting in August 2017, when the military launched a large-scale ethnic cleansing campaign against the Rohingya Muslim population in Rakhine State. More than 650,000 Rohingya have fled to neighbouring Bangladesh to escape mass killings, sexual violence, arson, and other abuses amounting to crimes against humanity by the security forces.

2017 marked the country's first full year under the democratically elected civilian government led by the National League for Democracy (NLD) and de facto civilian leader Aung San Suu Kyi. The NLD-led government took some positive steps, including ratifying the International Covenant on Economic, Social and Cultural Rights, engaging in some efforts to resolve past land confiscation cases, and enacting minor reforms to laws regulating speech and assembly. However, the government increasingly used repressive laws to prosecute journalists, activists, and critics for peaceful expression deemed critical of the government or military.

Despite the appearance of civilian rule, the military remained the primary power-holder in the country. It continued to block efforts to amend the 2008 constitution, which allows the armed forces to retain authority over national security and public administration through control of the defence, home affairs, and border affairs ministries. The constitutional provision allowing the military to appoint 25 percent of parliamentary seats affords it an effective veto over constitutional amendments.

The peace process with ethnic armed groups made no meaningful progress. Fighting intensified in Kachin and northern Shan States, resulting in an increase in forced displacement and other abuses against civilians, primarily by government forces.

Chapter - 4

Internal Security of China

The Chinese Communist Party (CCP) and State Council issued new guidelines on strengthening internal security in the wake of unprecedented terrorist attacks inside the country, rising public order concerns, and increasing online dissent. The guidelines called out the use of new high-technology and cyber-based assets, including data mining, closed circuit TV, and satellites, to help restore central government control. This is the first in a series of five brief items by Greg Austin, based on his 2014 book, Cyber Policy in China, providing some political context on how the country is using its cyber power in the service of internal security. See also the author's earlier post on how China will want to use artificial intelligence to support its internal security objectives.

China's recent economic woes have not weakened. Chinese President Xi Jinping's resolve to consolidate his authority in the country's three branches of power: the State Council, the Communist Party and the People's Liberation Army. In fact, Xi's military reforms and anti-corruption campaign have become all the more important, and it has also become clear that Xi will attempt to bring the vast, sprawling bureaucracy responsible for overseeing China's financial markets under his writ as well. For China, there is no distinction between internal and external security. Beijing's greatest fear is that outsiders will meddle in Chinese affairs if the cohesion of the regime breaks down. Maintaining discipline in the party and bringing the PLA to heel then are, in terms of security, no different than making sure that foreigners cannot take advantage of China's fiscal and monetary policy struggles.

On Jan. 11,2016, Xi convened both new and familiar leaders of the Chinese military, following a complete reorganisation of the PLA's command structure, and emphasised that they must "unswervingly follow" the orders and principles handed down by the Communist Party of China through the Central Military Commission. The next day, at the start of the Communist Party's Central Commission for Discipline Inspection's (CCDI) annual meeting, Xi stressed that discipline and party loyalty must be a step higher than the law. Also, on Jan. 12, sources told Reuters that the State Council was considering interim measures to manage its financial department until a new regulatory structure could be implemented. This came after numerous reports that Xi and the upper echelons of the Communist Party were displeased with last week's stock market snafu.

There are four key observations to make from these developments, all of which are interrelated. The first is that each of these events noted above deal with Xi cultivating personalised power in all of the three branches of power in China. The PLA is the ultimate guarantor of the regime's security, both internal and external. The Communist Party, which Xi is trying to make more efficacious and legitimate, is not just the founding and ruling political party of the People's Republic of China but is a complex organisation with 85 million members serving in both state and military organisations at every level. The State Council and China's other state institutions are closely linked to the Communist Party but ultimately represent the vast professionalised bureaucracy that implements party directives on more local levels. Xi is telling each institution that it must toe his line.

The second observation is that Xi continues to push forward in asserting the Communist Party's writ over the PLA. Rumours that discord was increasing between Xi and the military, along with the fact that many of the new commanders in the reformed military structure were in fact part of the previous structure and merely were moved around, suggest that Xi has had to compromise on at least some of his military reforms. Still, while many of the same faces remain in the PLA's leadership, the creation of 15 new functional departments out of the four that previously existed means Xi was able to add new faces personally loyal to him in the system. And now that the reorganisation is complete, Xi has wasted no time in stressing to all of these military leaders the importance of following orders and "discerning right from wrong." This is a tug of war between Xi and the PLA, and momentum will swing back and forward. Both sides have an interest in making sure the regime survives – but Xi is attempting to convince the PLA it has an interest, not just in the regime's survival, but in his own power.

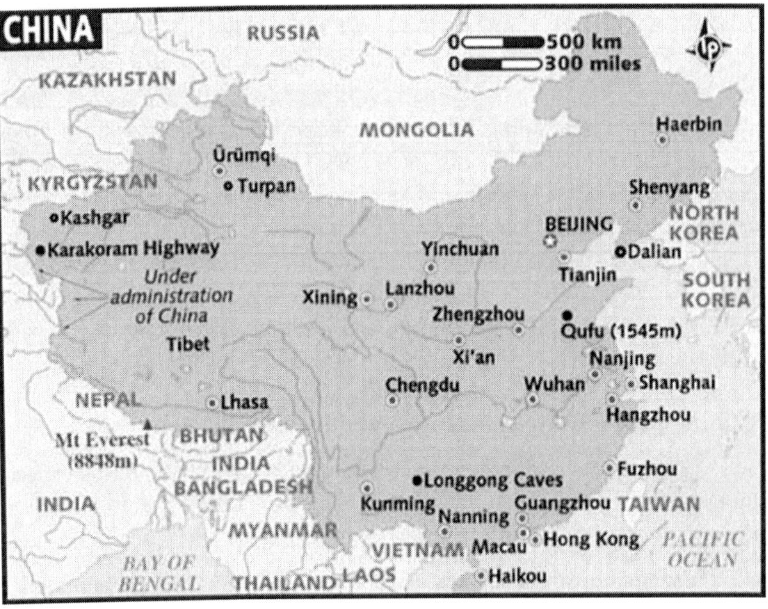

The third significant observation is Xi's personal involvement in the CCDI's continued anti-corruption investigations. The CCDI is an organ of the Communist Party and its anti-corruption purges are aimed at forging the party into a tool that Xi can use to implement central directives from Beijing throughout the country. The purges are also good for Xi's image and have created a popular image of Xi throughout China as a leader attempting to reinvigorate a structure that had become more concerned with personal advancement and wealth than with Communist Party principles or faithfully executing directives from the top leadership. An example of how the CCDI is accomplishing this can be seen in the announcement the disciplinary body made on Jan. 12, which stated that almost 34,000 party members had been subjected to discipline as a result of "frugality violations." These violations included the personal use of official vehicles and both giving and receiving bribes. What is most remarkable is the fact that this data is routinely collected via a monthly reporting system that the CCDI has established in Chinese provinces, state-owned enterprises and financial institutions. While the CCDI does not shy away from high-profile leaders, arguably its more important function is ensuring that Communist Party officials at the local level are maintaining discipline and loyalty.

Lastly, it is important to keep China's understanding of internal and external security in mind when understanding Chinese monetary policy. Last week, to add insult to the stock market injury, there was a sense both in China and in international markets that China's left hand didn't know what the right was doing. Circuit breakers put in place by the Chinese Securities Regulatory Commission (CSRC) had to be scrapped within four days of introduction because of the panic they induced on the Chinese stock market. Meanwhile, the People's Bank of China (PBOC) seemed to be giving mixed signals, pumping liquidity into the market while weakening the yuan's value against the U.S. dollar and largely remaining unresponsive to a gap that developed in onshore and offshore borrowing rates for the yuan.

China Spends Billions on Internal Security!

"China Spends Billions on Internal Security! China's domestic-security budget has surged to an astonishing $110 billion a year, larger than declared defence spending." The Economist. Let's look a little closer:

The Economist has never been very good with numbers (or economics) but that hasn't stopped them criticising China's economy and numbers. The Economist has predicted 56 'hard landings' for the Chinese economy since 1985 – while completely missing the Great Financial Crisis–and says China's $110 billion internal security budget shows that its government is insecure and terrified of its own people. Here's what it really shows:

- China spends $260 per capita (PPP) annually on internal security: police, prisons, fire departments, border patrol, forest service, gold mine and hydro security.
- The USA spends $670 per capita annually on internal security – excluding fire departments.
- Over three decades, state and local governments have tripled the amount spent on jails, compared to spending on education.
- Chinese police are unarmed.
- Chinese jails are relatively empty.
- China has very few repeat offenders.
- China has the safest streets in the world.
- China's internal security has the highest citizen approval in the world (90%).
- Chinese kids are better educated than American kids.

If we multiply the Chinese figure of $84 per person by 3 to account for the dollar's higher purchasing power in China, we find that China spends about $260 equivalent dollars. Perhaps that figure is lower because Chinese police are unarmed. This amount includes:

- All Fire Departments in China,
- The PAP (People's Armed Police),
- Border patrol,
- Forest service,
- Gold mine and hydro security.

Chapter - 5

Internal Security of Japan

The Japan Internal Security Forces is the Greater Empire of Japan's official, Empire-wide security force. The JISF's role is to maintain order in areas that have been recently annexed by The Empire, as well as to reinforce the Japanese Government's presence. The Japan Internal Security Forces are a paramilitary organisation. Unlike the Warrior Forces, JISF personnel use aging Western equipments.

History

The Japan Internal Security Forces were formed in 2031, after Taiwanese citizens began to riot in former Taipei. At the time, Daitai assets were working overseas, and did not have the capabilities to lend forces to the Japanese. As well, Japan could not make use of the Self Defence Forces or Riot Police without looking too brutish. Thus, a detachment of the Central Army's 3rd Division volunteered to form a paramilitary unit, which was named at the time Japanese Security Force of Taiwan. The Japanese Security Force of Taiwan also received some training and personal aide from the Central Reaction Force.

Later, realising that the Philippines would be next on the Daitai's chopping block, the Japanese Government began to merge volunteering police officers and military police officers into a single unit, which became the Japan Internal Security Force. The official JISF first saw action in Thailand in 2035, combating Islamic insurgents which had previously harassed the old Thai Government and Military. Japan Internal Security Forces fought insurgents mainly in Phuket, the former Thai countryside, and even had clashes with Islamic insurgents in Bangkok. The end result was a total Japanese victory, and the Islamic insurgency ended, with insurgents either killed in action or incarcerated.

The Japan Internal Security Forces left Thailand five years later, and began to serve in Vietnam, Laos, Cambodia, Malaysia, and eventually Australia. The Japan Internal Security Forces have received universal praise for their effectiveness at not only preforming paramilitary roles, but policing as well. Due to ongoing insurgencies, the JISF is deployed in former America, Canada, Russia, and China. Small detachments have been deployed in historically unstable prefectures to reinforce the presence of the Japanese Government.

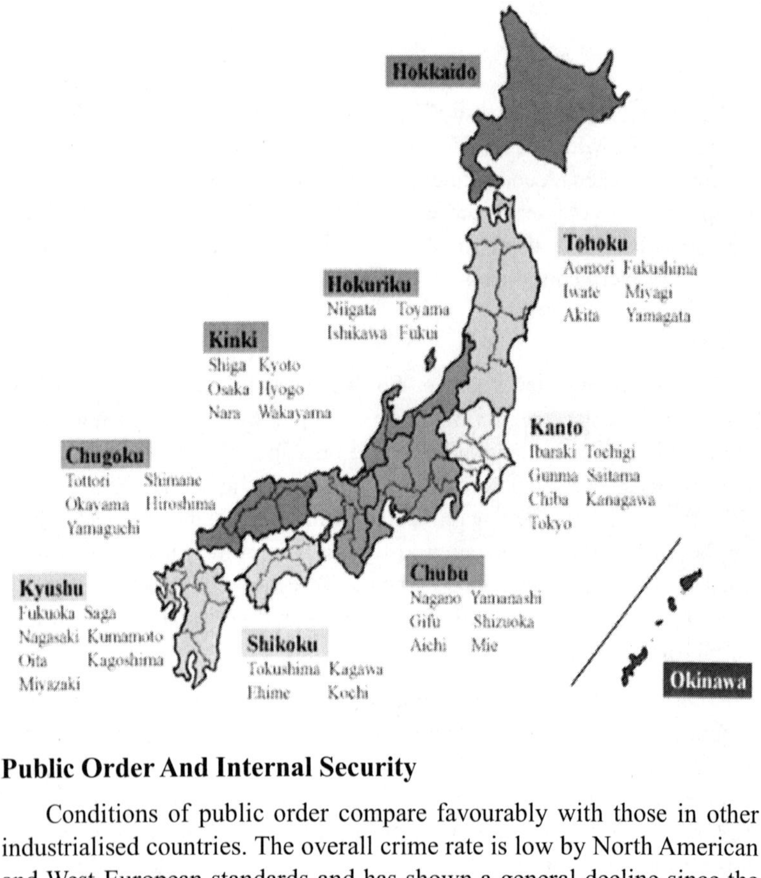

Public Order And Internal Security

Conditions of public order compare favourably with those in other industrialised countries. The overall crime rate is low by North American and West European standards and has shown a general decline since the mid-1960s. The incidence of violent crime is especially low, owing in part to effective enforcement of stringent firearms control laws. Problems of particular concern are those associated with a modern industralised nation, including juvenile delinquency, traffic control, and white-collar crime.

Civil disorders occurred beginning in the early 1950s, chiefly in Tokyo, but did not seriously threaten the internal security of the state. Far less frequent after the early 1970s, they were in all cases effectively countered by efficient and well-trained police units employing the most sophisticated techniques of riot control.

Japan's the police are an apolitical body under the general supervision of independent agencies, free of direct central government executive control. They are checked by an independent judiciary and monitored by a free and active press. The police are generally well respected and can rely on considerable public co-operation in their work.

Officials involved in the criminal justice system are usually highly trained professionals interested in preventing crime and rehabilitating offenders. They are allowed considerable discretion in dealing with legal infractions and appear to deserve the trust and respect accorded to them by the general public. Constitutionally guaranteed rights of habeas corpus, protection against self-incrimination, and the inadmissability of confessions obtained under duress are enforced by criminal procedures.

The prison system is generally modern and conducted from the viewpoint of re-socialisation. Prisoners are treated on an individualised basis, and education is emphasised. Special attention is given to juvenile offenders, who are normally housed separately from adult prisoners. A well-organised parole and probation program employs numerous citizen volunteers.

Japan's Security Policy in the Asia-Pacific during the post-Cold War Period

Despite domestic political changes, the alliance with the US continues to be the cornerstone of Japan's security policy in the Asia-Pacific region. Although Japan has taken some significant steps in the direction of normal statehood, the domestic constituency in favour of full strategic autonomy is still very weak. Japan's dilemma between its growing security concerns and the limitations laid by its Constitution will continue to be a major challenge in the coming years.

The Asia-Pacific region has now emerged as the main centre of dynamic economic and technological development in the world. Though the success story of Japan's rise to the status of an economic super power is too well-known, the growth trajectories of China and India , if their current tempo of growth is sustained, will add new dimensions to the emerging economic and security architecture of Asia as a whole.

One outstanding feature of the post-Cold War period is seen in the deepening of interdependence that is taking place among Asia-Pacific countries. There are strong trends towards economic integration as is evident by the conclusion of numerous free trade/economic partnership agreements and these will gather greater strength in the coming years as an efforts to build an Asian Community are accelerated. Multilateral bodies like the ASEAN, ASEAN+3, the ASEAN Regional Forum and APEC contribute to strengthen the trends towards regional integration. Many countries, which had earlier shunned multilateral security arrangements, have now changed their policies and today they are quite inclined to welcome them. However, the Asia-Pacific region is also very complex since it is home to diverse problems including those connected with territories, terrorism, ethnic and religious fundamentalism, nuclear proliferation, maritime security,and fierce competition for energy. Concerns over North Korea's nuclear weapons and ballistic missiles, and China's military modernisation, have also deepened. In addition, there are flash points like Taiwan that could flare up suddenly and destabilise the security situation of the region.

There are many aspects of Japan's security policy that need to be studied carefully. Despite domestic political changes, the alliance with the US still constitutes the cornerstone of Japan's security policy. Relations between Japan and the US have become more stable and balanced now and Tokyo has assumed several responsibilities, which it could not take up earlier. The rise of China and North Korea's nuclear and missile technology programme have increased the dependence of Japan on the US.

In the case of China, Japan has developed a strategy of engaging Beijing in both economic and political spheres. But since there is a great deal of volatility in their relations historical legacies, the dispute in the East China Sea on oil and gas resources and the territorial issue relating to the Senkaku islands Japan also believes in a policy of hedging against Beijing. North Korea is another major concern and Pyongyang's relentless pursuit of nuclear and missile technologies programme has deepened Japanese security concerns. Within Japan there is still no national consensus on amending Article Nine of the Constitution which has prevented Japan from assuming collective self-defence measures against external threats and as things stand now, there are no immediate prospects for any early constitutional change.

While keeping its security alliance with the US as an anchor, Japan has been making systematic efforts to increase its diplomatic options by moving closer to countries like India, Australia and the ASEAN Group. It is significant that Japan has signed declarations on security co-operation with India and Australia. Simultaneously, it has also expanded its military capabilities through a series of mid-term build-up programmes.

In the post-Cold War years, Japan's Self-Defence Forces have been playing an expanding role in the Indian Ocean region, Afghanistan and Iraq. Still, Japan is far from a position of exercising, its full strategic autonomy; until then, Japan's dilemma between its growing security concerns and the limitations laid by its Constitution will continue to be a major challenge. Japan will have to address this dilemma in the coming years if it wants to become a 'normal country'.

Chapter - 6

Internal Security of Nepal

A secure society is often understood as a civilised society. In a civilised society there is psychological assurance of security of life and property of individuals. But these are not the results of free gifts from the government. Behind these, there are sacrifices of the security forces. The security dilemma has been shifting from conventional military statecraft and is increasingly replaced by international relation, foreign policy, global governance and international security.

Hence, safety and security are the foremost pre-requisites and obligations of a sovereign nation. Changes in communication system and environment awareness have altered the world and Nepal too. Vision and behaviour of the leadership seem to be the same in Nepal, where injustice, insecurity and imbalance have prevailed.

Many committees were formed and their reports submitted, assurance of implementation was given but the people never sensed improvement. Emerging international issues of globalisation, diversity, environmental degradation, knowledge management, poverty, unemployment, food security, water-energy scarcity, infectious diseases, internal conflict, inter-state conflict, genocide, weapons of mass destruction, terrorism, ethnic conflicts, cybercrime, and human trafficking are terrifying countries like Nepal.

Issues of withdrawal of criminal cases pending in the courts; confusion about the role and implementation of Truth and Reconciliation Commission of Inquiry into Disappearances; mounting intensity of crimes; human trafficking, proliferation of small arms, illicit drug business, mushrooming INGOs; alarming prostitution, internally displaced persons; lack of responsiveness in post-earthquake management; immature diplomacy, disqualified Maoist militants — all these saddened the victims of Maoist insurgency, disappointed security personnel who escaped from regular forces; weak justice system, disputes among security agencies; rampant corruption, depressed conflict management, misuse of some mass medias; poor governance, brain-drain, youth-drain, transnational crimes and border encroachments are other critical dimensions and key loopholes.

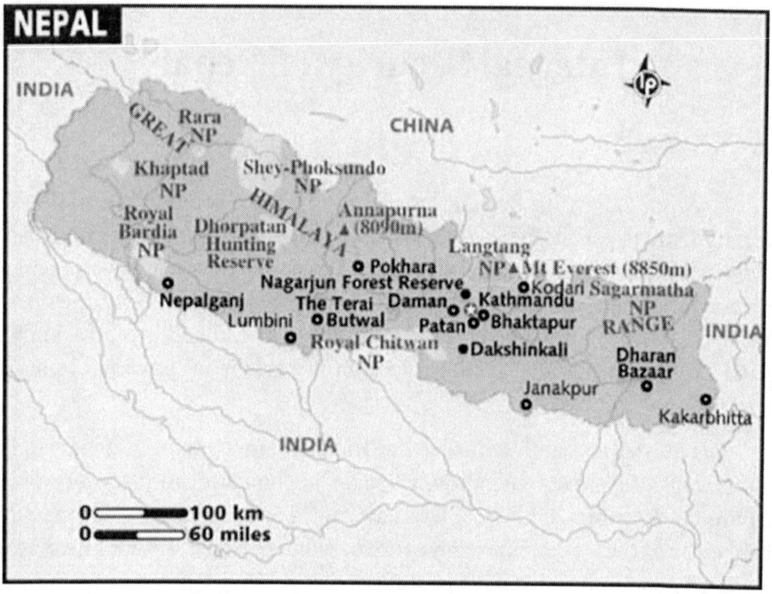

Nepal's democracy faces internal security challenges by a messy political legacy and shortfalls in professionalism. Qualitative decision making capacity, courage, and patriotism cannot be expected from an unprofessional command.

Various studies have found that there is the need of transformational leadership followed by participative/democratic, authentic and strategic models. The study sought the need of a system based policing 'intelligence-led' and 'police public partnership'.

Border issues along with imbalanced treaties must be managed with mutual benefit and understanding in the capacity of a sovereign nation. Federalism must not be interlinked with a particular community. One security force should not be an alternative to another but rather complementary.

Chiefs of police forces should be members of the National Security Council by the establishment of an "Internal Security Services Commission". "Security for sustainable development" as a shifting paradigm based on the principles of accountability, responsiveness, decentralisation, and empowerment could be a meaningful approach in security management. "SSRD: Security Sector Restructuring and Development" in terms of well defined laws, role and responsibility, procedure, operational mobility, deployment can be effective.

While rapid political changes took place, economic growth, national resources and the policy environment remain crippled by structural weaknesses and disjointedness; extreme inequalities; increasing the crisis of capacity and credibility.

The process of ideal change and development is complex but possible with the transformational leadership enhancing lasting peace, reliable security and sustainable development. Kathmandu, May 27, 2018: Minister for Home Affairs, Shakti Bahadur Basnet, said the government was preparing to introduce an internal security policy.

At a seminar entitled 'Effective Implementation of National Security Policy' organised by Former Police Council Nepal (FoPCON), Minister Basnet stressed on need for not only drafting the security policy but its effective implementation.

The country's current socio-economic and political scenario will be reflected in the security policy, Home Minister Basnet said, adding further it was essential that all the sectors adopted an equal perspective on Nepal's current scenario before implementing the national security policy.

FoPCON Vice Chairman and former Senior Superintendent of Police (SSP), Dr Chuda Bahadur Shrestha, said an extensive discussion in general should precede the implementation of the national security policy and act.

The seminar was attended by representatives of Nepal Police, Armed Police Force (APF), National Investigation Department Head, lawmakers, former police officials and officials of government authorities related to security. A working document on security issues was presented at the seminar.

Nepal Internal Security Consideration

Nepalese police, backed from time to time by the army, combat routine crimes in addition to monitoring numerous political strikes and demonstrations. The incidence of organised political violence was low, however. Nepal was not a fertile breeding ground for international terrorism because most political violence was committed by Nepalese dissidents to further their own domestic political agendas.

In the mid-1980s, small anti-monarchist and communist groups conducted a series of bombings in the Kathmandu Valley to dramatise their opposition to Birendra's rule. In June 1984, clandestine Maoist bands such as the Samyuktha Mukti Bahini (Socialist Liberation Army), the Democratic Front, and the United Liberation Torch Bearers mounted a campaign of bombings and assassinations intended to spark a revolution. Their actions had the opposite effect, however, as moderate opposition politicians condemned the violence and rallied around the king.

The opposition civil disobedience campaign was called off, and the Rashtriya Panchayat passed a stringent anti-terrorist ordinance to put down the threat. By August 1984, over 1,000 suspected terrorists and sympathisers were imprisoned under provisions of anti-terrorist legislation promulgated by the king.

The following year, another bombing in downtown Kathmandu killed eight persons and wounded twenty-two others. The sensational crime was perpetrated by the Jan Morcha (People's Front), a Taraibased antimonarchist group with ties to political thugs in the Indian border states of Uttar Pradesh and Bihar. Several Jan Morcha leaders who fled to India were convicted of the bombing in absentia. In June 1991, following the installation of the Nepali Congress Party government, King Birendra pardoned the exiled terrorists as a gesture of political goodwill.

The ethnic tensions that spilled across Nepal's international boundaries also posed security and foreign policy problems. In 1987 the Nepalese minority residing in the mountainous northern districts of the Indian state of West Bengal mounted a violent agitation demanding statehood within the Indian union for Indian citizens of Nepalese origins.

The standard bearer of the campaign was the Gorkha National Liberation Front led by Subhas Ghising, a former non-commissioned officer in an Indian Gurkha regiment. The communist state government of West Bengal complained of Nepalese collusion with the agitators after Ghising openly solicited Kathmandu's support and called on Gurkhas in the Indian Army to back the demand for a separate "Gorkhaland." The situation worsened when Indian police crossed the Nepalese border while pursuing Gurkha militants. Although Kathmandu probably was sympathetic to the plight of the Nepalese minority, any appearance of support for the statehood agitation was scrupulously avoided for fear of angering New Delhi. Official Nepalese support for the movement never was proven. By 1991 the Gorkhaland agitation had subsided after New Delhi, West Bengal, and Gurkha militants negotiated a political settlement that fell short of statehood.

Chapter - 7

Internal Security of Pakistan

Pakistan is a consociational society where different religious group are always in conflict with each other on petty issues. There are many horizontal and vertical cleavages in Pakistan that keep people divided on the basis of religion, caste, creed, status and language along with ever lasting lacuna between haves and have nots. These cleavages are not only undermining Pakistan's economic system but also causing socio-political CSS ForumsTuesday, June 12, 2018.

Pakistan's Internal Security Threats in the age of Globalisation

In this age of globalisation media has exacerbated the crisis and made Pakistan more vulnerable by disseminating disinformation, besides fabricated and manipulated stories that present a gloomy picture of the country and stop the foreign investment. Like other so-called political parties and leadership, media is also working against the national interest of Pakistan. Religious sectarianism is not a new phenomenon but it is an old saga. In ancient times, in Greece dichotomy was found between state and the church and then catholic and protestant sects were very popular in the West. In the same way subcontinent was also teemed with different sects and ethnic groups. This paper is going to give details about Pakistan's internal security threats regarding weak institutions, inefficient system capabilities, overlapping of political elite by non-political elite, media fabrications and non availability of honest leadership that make the system dysfunctional. Today all extremist elements are just showing their hatred against one man that is Pervaiz Musharraf and leading the country towards annihilation. This paper is based on optimism as I believe that we are sacrificing a lot after 9/11 and these sacrifices are taking Pakistan towards a destination that will make our next generations prosperous and happy.

In ancient Greece, there were conflicts between state and the church. In the West, controversies between Catholic and Protestant sects are found still today. Writing in the 19th century, William Carleton summed up what he thought was the essence of sectarianism:

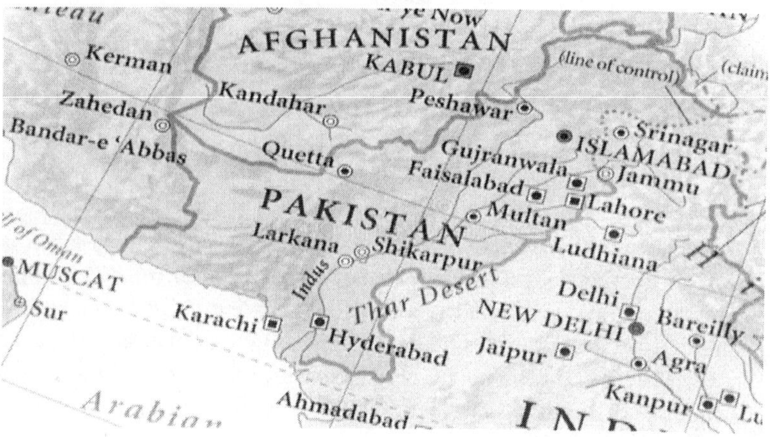

"If you hate a man for an obvious and palpable injury, it is likely that when he cancels the injury by an act of subsequent kindness, accompanied by an exhibition of sincere sorrow, you will cease to look upon him as your enemy; but when the hatred is such that while feeling it, you cannot on a sober examination of your heart, account for it, there is little hope that you will ever be able to stifle the enmity which you entertain against him."

Pakistan is a plural society. A number of peoples have been living in the country since independence (1947). Pakistan was attained on the basis of religion. Therefore, religion is considered important for ethnic groups, residing in Pakistan. Though Quaid- i-Azam believed that every individual in Pakistan would be free to live and worship according to the norms and values of his own religion. Untimely demise of the architect of Pakistan and assassination of the first premier pushed Pakistan into quagmire of crisis. It includes religious, linguistic, regional, provincial and cultural conflicts.

After independence, in 1947, different types of communities came to Pakistan. The government of Pakistan did its best to accommodate them according to the available resources.

Unfortunately, few people took the advantages of initial crisis and grabbed overeconomic and other land resources. They became the influential class of the country. This class wanted to keep its influence over other masses of the country. So, they decided to bifurcate the people into different clans, castes, linguistic and religious groups. Among these groups religion became the effective element to mobilise the people to have influence over the government and other institutions.

Therefore, so-called landlords exploited people in the name of religion. Later on, religion became a source of livelihood for some so-called ulemas. They decided to go on and exploited the name of religion for their multifarious objectives. In this way certain ethnic groups came into existence. Shia and Sunni are two major ethnic groups on the basis of religion, which have been conflicting with each other for last three decades of twentieth century.

The ethnic groups in Pakistan give rise to religious literature in which differences between Sunni sects have been mentioned. This religious literature causes conflicts in the country on sectarian basis.

In lieu of such crisis, provincial governments were directed to stop mosque sermons "against the faith of one sector or the other." Religious sectarianism emerged in Pakistan in Zia regime. In mid eighties a number of killings of Shias and Sunni groups were seen.

"Pakistani Sunni Muslims distinguish themselves into sects according to their school: Deobandi, Brelvi, Wahabi, Ahl-al- Hadith and so forth."

In this age of globalisation Pakistan is facing certain internal security threats. These threats are found at two levels:

1. National level
2. International level

In this paper we will only talk about **national level** security threats as such threats exposed Pakistan towards international threats. Present government assumed power in 1999 after throwing out Nawaz Sharief government and ruled the country with an iron hand. After 9/11 Pakistan considered as a front line state against terrorism. Perwaiz Musharaf became blue eyed boy for America. It transforms his defacto rule into dejure to an extent.

Contrary to this Pervaiz Musharaf became very much unpopular at home after his authoritative policies regarding ousting chief justice of Pakistan Supreme Court, Lal Masjid Massacre and worst ever energy crises along with rising dearness of consumer goods. On February 18, 2008, people of Pakistan showed hatred against president policies in general elections and did not cast vote in favour of Pakistan Muslim League (Q) group, a president's favourite party.

Therefore, today Pakistan is facing crisis in legitimacy of rule. President considers himself the chief exponent of all powers. Parliament urges to have its say in these prevailing crisis. Judiciary is totally helpless. Hence, internal security threats in Pakistan are not merely based on terrorism, extremism or any other religious ethnicity but it comprised of weak institutions, inefficient system capabilities, overlapping of political elite by non-political elite, media fabrications and non availability of honest leadership that make the system dysfunctional. Horse trading and floor crossing are such political upheavals that undermine a political system silently and make it futile in no time.

Security threats always increase when political system become dysfunctional. At present, Pakistan's political system is facing the worst phase of its history. Its system capabilities are at the state of abeyance and making it vulnerable.

Politically, Pakistan is very much unstable owing to its weak Political institutions, and low profile system capabilities. Jean Blondel defines them as: extractive, regulative, distributive, symbolic, and responsive. According to Blondel, extractive capability means that a political system should have the ability to extract its economic and natural resources at domestic and international levels. For example, collection of taxes at home and to bring more investments from abroad depicts that extractive capability is active. Regulative capability stands for the regulation of resources extracted both at home and abroad. Whereas distributive capability denotes the equitable distribution of the resources in the society obtained through extraction and regulation. First three capabilities directly relate to input function.

In the 'global village' environment this aspect of distribution resources is more attractive for direct investments from abroad and the quantum of exports, which indicate the effectiveness of distributive capability, symbolic capability, likewise, exposes the integration of a state through symbols, monuments, slogans, words and achievements. Whereas, responsive capability relates to the output function and demonstrates the system's response to the influx of demand coming from the public sector. This responsiveness' is always subject to the first four capabilities. If those capabilities are utilised timely and effectively, the response to the incoming demands will be adequately positive. But since all the capabilities relates to ever-changing domestic and global environments, they have their own implications making them variable.

Globalisation pierces into Pakistan's social, political and Economic systems. Luxury hotels; restaurants with power generators can be seen in different developed cities. Shops of personal computers, mobile phones, fax machines and Kodak colours with high speed one hour developing and printing service exist everywhere in Pakistan. It shows that western consumers have captured a lucrative market here and their ever available products have more value and credibility in this country. The country however, by itself though rich in computers and agriculture, lacks in electricity and water sources. A densely populated Pakistan, with heterogeneous culture and ethnic strife, seems to be another Yugoslavia of future.

Inefficient system capabilities are making Pakistan very much vulnerable at home. Alienation among common man is increasing owing to use of power against innocent and unarmed people by armed and uniformed men of the country. It created sentiments of hatred among people of the North and South Waziristan especially. Peoples living in other parts of Pakistan are also feeling insecure at home and aiming at men in uniform.

It is very painful that people of the same country are killing their fellow people. Media is another big reason of this security threat. Media is run by media conglomerates that have only one point agenda based on profit maximisation. Its fabricated and manipulated stories are helping extremist elements.It is causing migration of dreams and relative deprivation among common people also.

Luxurious life styles in their dramas, films and catchy advertisements attract people but their meager resources deny buying all that stuff, therefore they feel deprived and cause disturbance in the system. All three major institutions (Parliament, Judiciary and military) are unable to be professional in their approach. Media is also lacking the same element, so lack of professionalism, lack of stratified structures and lack of peoples' participation in Pakistan are reasons of increasing internal security threats.

Unfortunately, Pakistan lack professional politicians, we only have political demagogues who always convince people with their glib of tongue. Empirical study exposes that in our country both candidate and voter are selfish. Candidate always works for its election in the parliament by hook or crook and voter always casts the vote to the candidate who can go with him to police station at the time of his ordeal or could arrange a job for him or for his kins. This selfish attitude makes our system selfish that does not run for the welfare of the whole. It enhances individuality at local level and then at national level. It boosts provincialism that leads to extremism.

Religious ethnicity in Pakistan became at front in mid- eighties, when hardly a day went without the news of Sunni-Shia sectarian killings. The genesis of religious ethnicity in Pakistan can be found in different domestic and external perspectives and factors.

First a heterogeneous character of Pakistani society, where Muslims are predominant along with other minority groups like Christians, Sikhs Hindus, Parsis, and Ahmedis. All these communities are considered as religious ethnic groups in the country. Anti-Ahmedi riots in Pakistan in 1953 caused a serious threat to economic and political development of Pakistan. Zafarullah Khan and Mirza Ghulam Muhammad both were Qadianis and held higher official positions in government. In 1970s, Bhutto government declared the Ahmedis as minority ethnic group. It deprived them of certain rights. In the same way Hindus, Sikhs and Parsis are deprived of their rights. Parsis and Hindus are mostly found in Karachi. Ahmedis are mostly found in Rabwa. The structure of Pakistani society is divided among the different races and ethnic groups. The unbridled sectarianism, religious intolerance and ethnicity gave birth to non-political actors to act irrationally and in chauvinistic manners who also had very much influence in the peripheral areas of Pakistan. "At times, they seem to even challenge the authority of state and successive governments could not curb their activities."

Second, legacy of partition is an important and classical factor to understand the phenomenon of religious ethnicity in Pakistan. Pakistan came into existence in the name of Islam.

After the making of Pakistan, role of religion and Ulemas in the governance of the state remain unanswered. The successors like Liaquat Ali Khan, Mohammad Ali Bogra, Ghulam Mohammad etc.were all progressive and liberal personalities. They never gave any importance to

Ulemas and religion. The religious parties thus started demonstrations against the government.

Third, over emphasis on the Islamic character of state, also give rise to the religious ethnicity in Pakistan; from Quaid-i- Azam to present, every head of the state and head of government employed the name of religion for sustaining the rule. In the 1956 constitution, “the state was to be called Islamic Republic of Pakistan.” In 1960s, sectarian conflicts emerged but were confined to the Punjab. In 1961, Shia-Sunni riots circumscribed to a village, Tharhi, in the Khairpur, Mirs District of Sindh. The rest of the country remained intact of such conflicts.

Four, dichotomy between the educated elites and conservative Ulemas is another reason. Since, both belong to the same socio-economic and political conditions.Both are unable to create a unanimous solution for the development of the country because they are unaware about the real essence of religion and want to impose their own kind of religion which may be acceptable to one community but not to others.

Five, illiteracy among masses has compelled them to be exploited by the so-called Ulemas who are exploiting religion for their bread and butter. Innocent and ignorant masses are unaware about the reality of religion and easily start following the beliefs given to them by Ulemas and scholars. Ultimately their blind faith in Ulemas led them to ethnic conflicts that cause a heavy toll to their lives and belongings.

Six, Ijtehad is extinct in the present society that is the real source to appreciate the essence of Islam. Ijtehad is the source of Islamic laws, in which an individual does interpretation of certain problems in the light of laws of sharia according to his own reason. In Pakistan, the idea of Ijtehad is defunct. The so- called Ulemas do not accept any effort of Ijtehad in a real sense. Therefore, in the absence of any Mujtahid, the religion Islam can go hardly with the changing conditions.

“They instinctively rely upon the medieval Fiqah (law) manuals rather than understanding a fresh interpretation in the light of revealed sources. This attitude can be seen in a host of disputes regarding which items are subject to zakat and usher at which specific bodily point should be amputated, what the status and role of women should be in the Muslim society or how an Islamic economic system can be implemented.

Seven, human rights are not fully given to ethnic minorities in Pakistan. Christians, Parsis, Sikhs and Hindus are not given their due share in economic resources. It creates a sense of deprivation among the religious ethnic groups. Quota system has been introduced at provincial levels but religious ethnic groups have not been given a proper representation in the different departments of the government.

Eight,misinterpretation of religion is a major element that causes conflict among the religious ethnic groups which intentionally misinterpret the religious norms and values to keep them at daggers drawn.

Nine, foreign intelligence agencies cause religious ethnic conflicts in rival states like India, Afghanistan and Israel bribe certain religious ethnic groups in rival states and cause disintegration in those states. The Indian intelligence agency Research Analytical Wing (RAW) always indulges in performing destructive activities in Pakistan.

Ten, Pakistan's geopolitical contiguity has also caused religious ethnic conflicts. "The Zia regime (1977-88) coincided with the advent of the Islamic Revolution in Iran (1977 and onwards) and the Soviet military intervention in Afghanistan. For the first time in the history of Islam, Shia Ulemas took the reign of power in Iran." Pakistan's contiguity with Afghanistan, Russia, India and China has made the situation more complex for the religious ethnic groups. "The Ulemas had an access to the weapons and money after the soviet intervention in Afghanistan." Pakistan is teemed with sectarian and ethnic conflicts which are being created by religious scholars and their followers patronised by foreign powers like Iran on one hand and Saudi Arabia and Iraq on the other. Pakistan government also guesses the Indian hand in supporting Sipah-e-Sahaba against Shias and creating troubles in the country.

Sipah-e-Sahaba and Sipah-e-Muhamad were two ethnic militant groups, who had been conflicting with each other on the instance of foreign powers. One factor is much considerable that the Sunni school of thought is taught in academic institutions but Shia and other schools of thoughts are not allowed to be imparted in academic institutions so here conflict starts on the basis of sects.

In the pretext of such factors which cause rift among religiously united groups, certain implications can be observed which may cause threat to Pakistan's national security. Some observers consider Pakistan a vulnerable and meager state encompassed by the forces of religious ethnicity and sectarianism.

Ethnic conflicts are posing serious threats to our national security. Undoubtedly, threats were confined to Karachi. Sectarianism, which is the corollary of ethnic conflict, "poses horizontal threats to Pakistan's national security. The hot spots of sectarianism are not confined to a particular geographical region of the country. Shias and Sunnis all over the country feel threatened by fanatics of other sect whose number is on rise and have deadly weapons."

Religious ethnic conflicts can lead to the disintegration of the state and undermine the political and economic development of the country at a large scale. Religious ethnic groups run their own foreign and security policy agenda that is often does not correspond with the national security of Pakistan.

In the Indian held Kashmir, Jamait-e-Islami publicly supports Al Umer Mujahdeen and Hizb -ul-Mujahdeen. In 1988, Islami Ittehad of Nawaz Sharif and Jamait-e-Islami were supporting Sikh's right of self-determination in India. Russia also puts an allegation upon Pakistan's religious ethnic group Jamait-e-Islami, being involved in training Chechen rebels, striving for succession from Russian federation.China, fifty years old friend of Pakistan, scares about rebellion in Xinjan region as Uighur Muslims have good relations with Jamait-e- Islami since 1960s. In this context China has denied to open the second route to Central Asia through Kirgysistan.

Another classical example can be seen in this respect; Chinese Presidents Jing Zemain and Hu Jintao visited India and Pakistan in 1996 and 2006 respectively, suggested that both India and Pakistan should resolve Kashmir dispute through bilateral negotiations. It shows the changed attitude of China in the backdrop of Jamait-e-Islami's support to Muslims in Xinjian province.

Therefore, above-mentioned examples categorically reveal that internal security threats along with religious ethnicity is pushing Pakistan towards the diplomatic isolation and increasing the crisis more rapidly. Not only the national security is endangered by the religious ethnicity but political and economic developments are also being marred by their activities inside and outside the country.Foreign investment never comes to a country where fundamental groups seem active in the country. Therefore unemployment rises on one hand and industrialisation and modernisation stop on the other that are sine qua non for sustainable human development.

Religious elements flourish when state stop performing its Duties. The incidents like Lal Masjid and Maulana Fazlullah started preaching Islam through an illegal establishment of an FM radio.Why the authorities remain silent at the time of launching that radio? In the same way why Lal Masjid extremists allowed to established? All these examples prove that government remains dormant and unable to perform its functions in time. Therefore we have to face the music.

In this age of globalisation people are very much aware of each and every thing.It is almost impossible for the people to keep them ignorant from facts. It is an open secret today that Pakistan has been indulged in taking dictation from America and its allies that made the Musharraf regime unpopular among the people and lost general elections in February 2008.This is the positive side of media that articulates the public opinion but when it sensationalises the facts and distorts reality, it becomes a crime.

Media did well in exposing dictatorial activities of the Pervaiz Musharaf regime and kept them at heals during judicial crisis.Government became aware that authoritarianism and concentration of power can not win hearts of the people. Flour crisis, energy crisis, no rule of law, no social justice, unemployment, dearness have made our system dysfunction. The status of system capabilities is at the lowest ebb. Recommendations to curb internal security threats in Pakistan.

Pakistan is a country where different types of people have been living together for a long time.Government of Pakistan should try to understand the basic needs of different religious ethnic groups and should provide them opportunities accordingly.The economic resources of the country should also be shared equally as to satisfy the demands of all, lead them to assimilate themselves in the main stream of the country. These majority groups are not ready to amalgamate with other ethnic groups.

In Pakistan, Ahmedis are never welcomed by Sunni Muslims therefore; rift between them can hardly be eliminated but minimised by fulfilling their needs and demands in time.

President of Pakistan is very much concerned with the ethnic concerns in Pakistan that is why he has given much liberty to the press and media to hold debates and open discussions for maximum information and awareness to the people.

Pakistan is a consociational society where different religions are found on different life styles. Undoubtedly, Musharraf government is doing its best to curb religious sectarianism in Pakistan. The reforms include ban on different extremist religious parties,supervision of Mudrassas, and change in curriculum and syllabus in different grades. The U.S. government is still unsatisfied with the reforms and consistently forcing the government to have check on extremist elements in Pakistan and its surroundings. The executive summary of the U.S. also talks about Hudood Ordinances and government efforts to create a moderate environment in the country.

Matter of the fact is that Pakistan has done much better reforms to curb ethnicity. Pervaiz Musharraf himself at stake owing to his reforms for religious tolerance and enlighten moderation.He is really "in the line of fire" after his policies for mudrassas,change of syllabus in text books, women protection bill,Lal Masjid massacre, Waziristan dilemma,rift with judiciary and many other that all based on pursuing U.S interests. As Musharaf himself accepted in a private TV Channel programme that "yes he had been under pressure," that pressure definitely put upon by the U.S.

Conclusion

In Pakistan,religion is always politicised to legitimize the rule of the ruler. That is why religion can never become binding force in Pakistan. It is not the fault on the part of the religion but wrong doers are those who have indulged in worldly affairs unable to work for the welfare of the whole. They always have their own axe to grind and exploit the unevenness in the country for attaining their nefarious objectives. Allah says in Quran, "Do not call names who call others as their omnipotent except me." Allah is himself saying no religious ethnic group should be allowed to abuse any other religious ethnic group of the country. So we are not supposed to abuse anyone's religion, as this is the real essence of Islam in which tolerance is preferred. Equality, fraternity and justice are other pristine canons of Islam, which unite the society for good. No religion in the world preaches killing and destruction. It is high time for us to consider that panacea of all our ills lie in developing democratic institutions, specialisation of functions, sustainable human development that are only possible in good governance that can only be achieved through independence of judiciary and rule of law.

Tolerance towards other communities is sine qua non for all individuals. It will boost national consensus and enhance solidarity among peoples. On the part of the state it is indispensable to perform its duties efficiently without any biased and egoistic approach. Until or unless rule of law is not observed in Pakistan internal security threats will remain even in this age of globalisation.

Chapter - 8

Internal Security of Sri Lanka

The National Security Council of Sri Lanka is the executive body of the Sri Lankan government that is charged with the maintenance of national security with authority to direct the Sri Lankan military and Police. It was established in 1999.

On June 11, 2018, a US Congress delegation from the House Armed Services Committee, told President Maithripala Sirisena that internal security of Sri Lanka is important for regional security and world peace.

The delegation, which included the Chairman of the House Armed Services Committee, Mac Thornberry, Henry Cuellar, Vickie Hartzler and Carol Shea-Porter, met President Sirisena in Colombo today. During the meeting, the President said that Sri Lanka will work with the international community and recalled the assistance given by the US in training the Sri Lankan security forces, the President's office said

Military training programmes are being conducted between the US and Sri Lanka routinely, the President said, pointing out the necessity of using more technological knowledge to further promote these programmes, and emphasised that there is no defence without the technology in the modern world.

President Sirisena said that the co-operation of the United States Security forces is important to control the ways that drugs are smuggled into the country and for that the co-operation between countries is also of utmost importance.

The Congress committee members agreed to provide assistance to prevent drug trafficking in Sri Lanka and added that it is their country's policy to give necessary assistance in order to build Sri Lanka as a strong and prosperous country.

Secretary to the President Austin Fernando, Secretary to the Ministry of Foreign Affairs Prasad Kariyawasam and the Ambassador of the United States to Sri Lanka Atul Keshap also attended the meeting. **(Colombo Gazette)**

Giving an elaborate perspective of National Security concerns and challenges ahead, the War Hero, Major General Udaya Perera, Commander, Security Force Headquarters - Kilinochchi (SFHQ-KLN) during the day's (Wednesday 4th) Session One of the ongoing 'Defence Seminar - 2013' identified regional, global and national threats as far as Sri Lanka's security is concerned.

Here follows the full text of his comprehensive presentation;

"Sri Lanka is the only country in the contemporary world which was able to comprehensively defeat a hybrid Terrorist movement once recognised as the most deadliest and ruthless which bleed the nation for almost three decades involving in a protracted separatist campaign. Today Sri Lanka is enjoying the full benefit of violence free environment, steadily moving towards permanent peace and stability despite countless attempts by many actors to destabilise it once again. The success was mainly due to enduring national will to defeat separatism orchestrated by charismatic political leadership. Countless sacrifices of tangible and intangible resources, wining over feelings of mistrust, inculcating tolerance over hate and forgiveness led to harness the national will in support of the common goal of defeating terrorism. The strength of our resilient nation is the ability to forgive and forget traumatised past with the hope of looking towards a better future in a harmonious society. Nevertheless anti social and anti Sri Lankan elements are at a countless struggle to tarnish the hard won victory over terrorism by haunting the past undermining the sovereignty and territorial integrity of our nation. Therefore it could be stated that Sri Lanka still encounters an active potential threat from varied sources. Protecting the state and the nation against these threats is the foremost responsibility of the Government and its defence forces. A comprehensive National Security Strategy to pursue the nation's interest without any impediment is the foundation of a progressing country in attaining prosperity and sustainable peace. It is the enduring right of any sovereign state to formulate its National Security Strategy to safeguard its national interest by considering strategic threat environment. As Lord Palmerston said "Nations have no permanent friends or allies, they only have permanent interests" is more relevant in today's context. This implies every sovereign nation whether big or small, strong or weak, developed or undeveloped has the right to peruse its national interests for the best advantage of the nation without being a threat to another, and every other nation shall respect the "fair and just" national interests that every sovereign has the right to peruse. However, conflicts of interests are very common in this Volatile, Uncertain, Complex and Ambiguous international environment that may lead to dissatisfaction and disputes amongst nation states. Therefore, Diplomacy, diplomacy and diplomacy is foremost national power in dealing with potential triggers, through bilateral and multilateral diplomatic engagement to avoid conflict and military should be in full readiness to mitigate and face unavoidable and unforeseen threats and challenges.

With that as the background I will now proceed to very briefly identify common global threats and challenges and then discuss new trends, challenges and concerns on national security of Sri Lankan in post-conflict context.

Common Global Threats and Challenges:

The common global security threats could be analysed under broad categories as depicted on the screen:

a. Nuclear.
b. Biological.
c. Cyber.
d. Environment and Climatic Changes and Natural Disasters.
e. Transnational Crime.
f. Terrorism.

Nuclear

After the Cold war and with the disintegration of erstwhile USSR, the traditional nuclear competition and the threat of nuclear race have reduced drastically. However, large stockpiles of nuclear arsenals remain with nuclear nations including in our neighbourhood raising security concerns. Further, as nuclear disarmament is a dream and non-proliferation is unrealistic the conventional nuclear threat will continue to remain. However, a more likely contemporary threat would be a low-yield "dirty bomb" in the hands of terrorists.

In Sri Lankan context proximity of nuclear facilities of peaceful purposes may pose a threat due to the possibility of a leak as in the case of Fukushima nuclear plant in the year 2011. Threats of this nature cannot be ignored or ruled out especially due to scale and frequency of natural disasters owing to climatic change.

Biological Threats

Countering Biological Threats with an underlying theme that biological weapons eventually will be used in a terrorist attack is a possibility that should be catered in national security strategy where Sri Lanka land forces should be capable to deal with.

Cyber

The drumbeats of cyberwarfare have been sounding for years. Network intrusions are widely viewed as one of the most serious potential challenges to national security, public safety and to economic domain. Technology, in this case, becomes a double-edge sword. It is becoming more and more clear that the increasing persistence and sophistication of cyber attacks will require solutions beyond the traditional.

Emergence of technology driven new media including social media sites such as Facebook, Twitter and other websites on the Internet, operating in the cyber domain has also become a threat to national security. We have seen the potential of this new media to destabilise nations and affect serious change in the case of countries like Tunisia, Libya, and Egypt. Although the likelihood of events such as the Arab spring transpiring in Sri Lanka is extremely remote, it being a matured democracy with an extremely popular political leadership, this is yet another threat that needs to be monitored. As per research conducted by IT and social science professionals, the category called the NEETs, personnel Not in Education, Employment or Training, a segment of youth who idle are the largest community of youngsters globally and locally that engages in activities in the web on which intelligence community need to keep a close watch.

Transnational Organised Crimes

Law-enforcement agencies world over, see transnational criminal networks as national security challenges. These groups cause instability and subvert government institutions through anti-social activity in collaboration with local underworld. Transnational criminal organisations have accumulated unprecedented wealth and power through the drug trade, arms smuggling, human trafficking, and other illicit activities that exceed 50 in number. They extend their reach by forming alliances with terrorist groups. Even advanced sophisticated technology in developed countries is not nearly enough to counter this threat. The way forward is through intelligence sharing and co-operation between law enforcement authorities and defence establishments.

Terrorism

According to Bruce Hoffman, all terrorists share one common denominator; they "live" in the future, and are convinced that they will defeat their enemies". Sri Lanka gave a strong message to terrorists that live in the future and proved they are not indispensable. Sri Lanka proved beyond doubt that terrorism can be defeated with a well articulated whole of government strategy and a well focused charismatic political leadership.

As per David C Rapport, the world has experienced for waves of modern terrorism starting from late 19th century. They are Anarchist, Anti-colonial, New Left and the last and most ferocious the Religious/Ethnic wave. Sri Lanka bravely faced last three waves while comprehensively defeating the New Left Wave and the Ethnic Wave. While third wave was more of insurgency and the fourth was Hybrid Terrorism practically and by definition. Dr Tom Marks explains the difference being " in insurgency Terrorism is a Tactic and Terrorism is a logic in classic Terrorism. In hybrid terrorism, terrorist groups go beyond Tactics and Logic and employ conventional and other means of warfare to achieve political ends.

LTTE at the time of confronted by the state in the year 2006 had established a counter state in North and East of Sri Lanka controlling a land mass of 1300 Sq Km. They also boasted of maintaining a so-called Army, Navy, Air Force and other institutions that are required for a state entity. This hybrid Terrorist outfit was comprehensively defeated, firstly, by isolating it globally, regionally and locally through the elements of national power and "isolated LTTE" received the final death blow from the Military, as depicted on the screen. Taking David's Wave theory together with Huntingtons theory of clash of civilisations as the global conflict in the offing, NSS should ought to focus on a possible fifth wave which may be a Tsunami than a wave if not prevented.

There are elements that are propagating the fifth wave internationally which will be discussed subsequently. In the present context international community should be mindful of hybrid terrorism being spread through networks of attachments and prevent the fourth wave being transformed to the fifth.

Challenges and Security Threats due to Environmental and Climate Change and Natural Disasters:

The national security ramifications of climate change are severe. Although the topic of climate change has been hugely politicized, issue should be considered as a serious security crisis. In the 21st century, we recognise that climate change can impact national security - ranging from rising sea levels, to severe droughts, to the melting of the polar caps, to more frequent and devastating natural disasters that raise demand for humanitarian assistance and disaster relief. Change created by a warming planet will lead to new conflicts over refugees and resources. Catastrophic natural disasters can also lead to severe leaks of radioactive material and poisonous gases, all these would require increased military support which is considered in our strategy.

New Trends, Challenges and Concerns on National Security of Sri Lanka in Post Conflict Context:

Threats specific to Sri Lanka's National Security are mainly of unconventional nature imposed by non-state actors and proxies. This situation could be further evaluated under following broad categories as depicted on the screen:

(a) Ideological Threat and International Network.

(b) Threats from Non State Actors.

(c) Destabilisation through constituting ethnic and religious enclaves.

(d) Perception.

Ideological Threat and the International Network:

Most severe threat to NS derives from separatist ideology through the facilitation of pro LTTE international network. Though LTTE was completely defeated locally the international network is becoming more and more active due to support they enjoy from regional extremist political entities that share similar ethnic sentiments and the Tamil diaspora. Some international state and non-state actors too are supporting through persuasion and for local political gains. Many major cities in the world and some capitals are with ethnic enclaves that can influence constituencies to a great extent through lobbying and political manoeuvring. Local politicians in these constituencies may not be able ignore the influence of these naturalised Tamil elements in their political campaigns and in power politics. While Organisations that were active during the period of conflict in supporting the LTTE politically, financially and morally continues to propagate the ideology some more organisations with leading LTTE members who left the country during last stages of military humanitarian operation have mushroomed in the international scene to continue the ideological campaign. Organisations such as TGTE, BTF, MTF, HQ GP and TCC work as a closely knitted network with GTF under Fr Emmanuel as the hub. These organisations are capitalising on the vulnerability of Tamil economic refugees for their advantage. While some governments are supporting these elements based on false propaganda some states turn a blind eye giving excuses such as their domestic laws do not permit any action against such organisations.

This attitude of nations will never deter global terrorism, rather will blossom. James J Carfarno clearly identifies such states in his book "how to win the long war" as Aggressors, Enablers and Slackers. Therefore threat to National Security is not only from organisations that carry the ideology but also from aggressor, enabler and slacker nations.

Global Tamil Forum (GTF), the centric network of organisations has successfully influenced a number of politicians from various political parties in European countries as well as the United States, Australia, Canada, and India to support the separatist Ideology. In addition, the GTF has courted officials within international organisations such as the United Nations, the

European Union and various international non-governmental organisations to obtain their support. Therefore Sri Lanka needs the support of the international community to deal with organisations that seek not only to challenge the sovereignty and integrity of our nation but also to breed terrorism with separatist ideology.

Destabilising the Nation by Creation of Ethnic and Religious Enclaves:

Internationally active groups with a separatist ideology such as GTF, BTF, TCC, HQ Gp and TGTE is vying for a separate state through a well orchestrated strategy, initial step being creating and strengthening of Ethnic enclaves. LTTE terrorists did this through ethnic cleansing and GTF and TGTE is doing it by exerting international pressure to the Sri Lankan Government for constitutional changes by lobbying foreign governments. Some governments are exerting pressure on the Govt of Sri Lanka to legalise the process without anticipating the threat posed by such moves to national and regional security.

Threats from Non State Actors

Non-state actors and entities are of basically two categories. They are violent and non violent. Violent non-state actors include terrorist, insurgent and violent extremists groups that were discussed earlier under the heading terrorism. Threat from non-violent non-state actors comes from INGOs, and NGOs who work on a hidden agenda to destabilise the sovereign state of Sri Lanka. I need to go back to the history, to the 17th century. Treaty of Westphalia was signed in 1648 to bring in amity and promote the state as the most prominent and most influential actor in world politics. For the first time in the history of the world.

Westphalia Treaty recognised the principle of the sovereignty of nation states, secondly the principle of equality between nation states, thirdly the principle of internationally binding treaties between states and fourthly the principle of non-intervention of one state in the internal affairs of the other. In short the Peace of Westphalia believed that there is nothing more important than the sovereignty of a state. However 21st century has taken a different turn where day-by-day state sovereignty is diluting giving way to non state entities with their wealth and influence to dictate terms to states. This dangerous trend if not checkmated will lead to creation of weak states and ungoverned spaces where violent non-state actors could be active creating an unsafe world.

Perception

Sri Lanka post-war environment is marked by the Government's strong focus on economic development, including reconstruction of the war-affected areas. Against this backdrop, the Government lifted the emergency regulations in September 2011 while reiterating a threat to Sri Lankan sovereignty posed by the activity of the TGTE, BTF, GTF, and other transnational separatist organisations that are regularly having links and deals with foreign parliamentarians and heads of international organisations. These groups form the core for separatism. They are responsible for strong lobbying on issues of accountability and human rights violations by distorting facts. This includes manipulating information, communicating false information, propagating deceptive information and communications designed to distort the perception of the international community and the local Tamil population regarding government policies, ranging from international issues to domestic politics. The TNA Political campaign for the Northern Provincial Council Elections to be held in September this year is based on these lines and is funded by these organisations and part of the Diaspora that wage a perception campaign against the Government of SL. Therefore perception management through a diplomatic and information campaign essentially form part of the National Security strategy and Army too has a role to play.

Conclusion

The above Security Concerns related to Sri Lankan National Security encompasses a number of challenges the state need to address in the post conflict scenario to ensure sustainable peace. The government's grand strategy in the post conflict scenario is based on 5Rs in achieving sustainable peace and development for which the Sri Lankan Army plays a major role.

In a post conflict scenario state intelligence services have a major role to play in identifying new threats in order to revisit and shape and reshape to meet the challenges of complex and ever-changing security environment. The Sri Lanka Army, together with its Intelligence arm as the largest military component is fully engaged in achieving sustainable peace and also fully prepared to meet challenges to national security in the post-conflict environment by closely monitoring new trends."

Chapter - 9

Internal Security of France

The General Directorate for Internal Security (French: Direction générale de la sécurité intérieure, DGSI) is a French intelligence agency. It is charged with counter-espionage, counter-terrorism, countering cybercrime and surveillance of potentially threatening groups, organisations, and social phenomena.

The agency was created in 2008 under the name Central Directorate of Interior Intelligence (French: Direction centrale du renseignement intérieur, DCRI), merging the direction centrale des Renseignements généraux (RG) and the direction de la surveillance du territoire (DST) of the French National Police. It acquired its current name in 2014, with a small structural shift: contrary to the DCRI which was part of the National Police, the DGSI reports directly to the Ministry of the Interior.

The DGSI is headed by General Director Patrick Calvar. The agency is informally known as the "RG", a nickname formerly used for the Direction centrale des renseignements généraux which merged into it.

This is a list of current and former **French intelligence agencies.**

Currently active

DGSE: Directorate-General for External Security – Direction générale de la sécurité extérieure. It is the military foreign intelligence agency, which succeeded the Service de Documentation Extérieure et de Contre-Espionnage (SDECE) in 1982 (itself preceded by the Direction Générale des Études et Recherches (DGER), dependent on the BCRA.

DGSI: General Directorate for Internal Security – Direction générale de la sécurité intérieure. Founded in 2008 by the merger of the RG and the DST, it is tasked with counter-espionage, counter-terrorism and the surveillance of potential threats on French territory.

DRM: Directorate of Military Intelligence – Direction du renseignement militaire. It was created by Socialist Interior Minister Pierre Joxe in 1992, after the Gulf War, to centralise military intelligence information.

DPSD: Directorate for Defence Protection and Security – Direction de la protection et de la sécurité de la défense. It is a military intelligence agency, charged with conducting counter-espionage.

BRGE: Intelligence and Electronic Warfare Brigade – Brigade de renseignement et de guerre électronique.

DCPJ: Judicial Police – Direction centrale de la police judiciaire.

CNCIS: National Commission for the Control of Security Interceptions – Commission nationale de contrôle des interceptions de sécurité.

SCRT: Central Service of Territorial Surveillance - Service central de surveillance du territoire.

Former agencies

Bureau Central de Renseignements et d'Action (BCRA) was an intelligence agency created during World War II in 1940.

Deuxième Bureau: France's external military intelligence agency from 1871 to 1940. It was dissolved together with the Third Republic upon the armistice with Germany.

DST: Directorate of Territorial Security – Direction de la surveillance du territoire. It was an intelligence agency of the Minister of Interior, charged with conducting counter-espionage (in particular in economic matters), and, since the end of the Cold War, also with counterterrorism issues. It was abolished in 2008 and merged into the DCRI.

RG: General Intelligence Directorate – Direction centrale des renseignements généraux. It was the intelligence agency of the French police, directed by the Minister of the Interior. It was charged with overlooking gambling activities, criminal activities, and political radicals (far right and far left). It also used to have as a mission to oversee French political parties, but officially is not charged with this anymore. It was merged into the Direction centrale du renseignement intérieur in 2008.

Service de documentation extérieure et de contre-espionnage (SDECE)), successor to BCRA.

Reinforcing internal security and the fight against terrorism

The Act to reinforce internal security and the fight against terrorism was promulgated by the President of the Republic on Monday 30 October 2017. Its provisions are aimed at preventing terrorist acts while preserving individual liberties.

The Act contains four key measures:

1. **Establish protection perimeters in order to ensure security at events or in particularly vulnerable places** (such as sports and cultural events). The Prefect will be able to authorise visual bag inspections and security frisking by private security agents, under the supervision of police officers and gendarmes. Internal security forces will also be able to search vehicles with the consent of the driver. If any person does not submit to checks, he or she will be denied access or removed from the security perimeter.
2. **Allow the closure of places of worship** when "words, writings, activities, ideas or theories" that incite or endorse terrorism, and incitement "to hatred and discrimination" are used there. In order to regulate the use of this power, a prior adversarial procedure is provided for as well as a time limit which shall be no less than 48 hours, allowing an interim order application to be lodged before an administrative judge.
3. **Allow the administrative authority to put in place administrative controls and individual monitoring** measures against any person in respect of whom there is serious reason to believe their behaviour constitutes a "particularly serious" threat and who enters into regular contact with individuals or organisations with terrorist intent or who supports or adheres to views that incite terrorism. This measure is less restrictive than house arrest, but is sufficient to ensure effective monitoring. It may be accompanied by the obligation to report once a day to the police or gendarmerie units and may be renewed for three months if new or additional information is presented (within a limit of 12 months). The person may be exempted from this daily obligation to report if they agree to be placed under electronic surveillance. Anyone subject to these measures will be obliged to provide their e-mail login details and subscriber numbers.

4. **Allow Prefects to order, only with the prior authorisation of the judge supervising releases and detention, the entry and search of any place** if there is serious reason to believe it is being frequented by a person posing a terrorist threat or who is in contact with such persons.

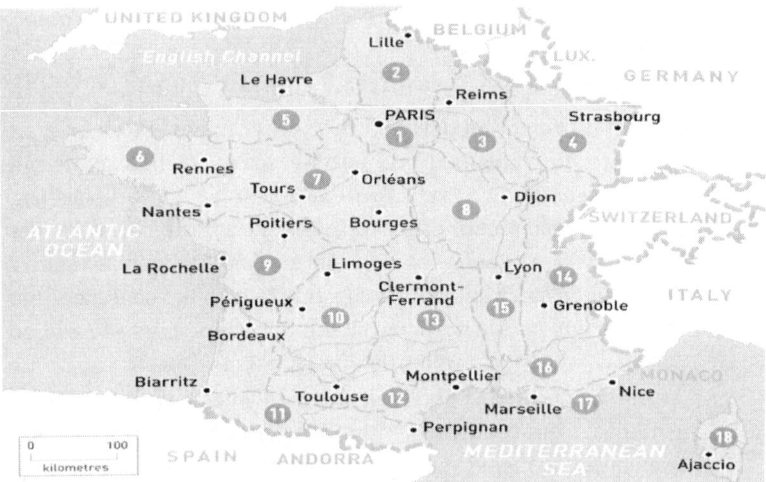

In order to prevent the terrorist threat more effectively, there are two important additional measures.

- The ability to carry out administrative investigations for civil servants in positions of authority and who pose a risk of radicalisation, and where necessary, to take appropriate action, either by transferring, suspending or removing the person(s) concerned.
- The ability to carry out identity checks in border areas or within a 10km radius of airports and international stations. This provision will grant "the ability, when the risk is known to be real and imminent, to arrest individuals who are likely to commit attacks on French soil", said Gérard Collomb during the press conference of 30 October 2017.

The Act also provides for further measures.

- Adapt French law to the Passenger Name Record (PNR). This record lists all air and sea passengers entering or leaving French space, so that the movement of individuals who pose a threat can be detected more easily (learn more by reading: "Adoption of the PNR").

- Extending the duration and scope of control possibilities in border areas. The text allows for possible identity checks "around railway stations" (not just inside them as before) as well as "within a maximum radius of twenty kilometres around [the most sensitive international] ports and airports". It also provides for the maximum duration of a check to be increased from six to twelve hours.
- Introducing a new legal system for surveillance of wireless communications.
- Extend the scope and duration for carrying out checks in border areas. Article 19 reinforces the current provision:
  - by extending the maximum duration of checks from 6 to 12 hours,
  - by allowing checks to be carried out around international stations,
  - by extending the ability to conduct such checks around certain border crossing points (ports and airports) chosen because of the large number of people travelling through them and their vulnerability within a boundary limit of 10 kilometres.
- Establish a new legal regime for monitoring wireless communications. Articles 15 and 18 of the Act establish a legal framework for operations to monitor wireless communications.
- The creation of a new criminal offence carrying a 15-years prison sentence and a fine of €225,000 for parents who incite their children to commit acts of terrorism or travel abroad for that purpose, is provided for in Article 10; this sentence may be accompanied by the loss of parental authority.

Chapter - 10

Internal Security of Russia

The Federal Security Service of the Russian Federation is the principal security agency of Russia and the main successor agency to the USSR's Committee of State Security (KGB). Its main responsibilities are within the country and include counter-intelligence, internal and border security, counter-terrorism, and surveillance as well as investigating some other types of grave crimes and federal law violations. It is headquartered in Lubyanka Square, Moscow's centre, in the main building of the former KGB. The Director of the FSB since 2008 is general of the army Alexander Bortnikov.

The immediate predecessor of the FSB was the Federal Counterintelligence Service (FSK) of Russia, itself a successor to the KGB: on 12 April 1995, Russian president Boris Yeltsin signed a law mandating a reorganisation of the FSK, which resulted in the creation of the FSB. In 2003, the FSB's responsibilities were widened by incorporating the previously independent Border Guard Service and a major part of the abolished Federal Agency of Government Communication and Information (FAPSI). The two major structural components of the former KGB that remain administratively independent of the FSB are the Foreign Intelligence Service (SVR) and the State Guards (FSO).

Under Russian federal law, the FSB is a military service just like the armed forces, the MVD, the FSO, the SVR, the FSKN, Main Directorate for Drugs Control and EMERCOM's civil defence, but its commissioned officers do not usually wear military uniforms.

The FSB is mainly responsible for internal security of the Russian state, counterintelligence, and the fight against organised crime, terrorism, and drug smuggling. Since 2003, when the Federal Border Guards Service was incorporated to the FSB, it has also been responsible for overseeing border security.[1] The FSB is engaged mostly in domestic affairs, while espionage duties are responsibility of the Russian Foreign Intelligence Service. However, the FSB also includes the FAPSI agency, which conducts electronic surveillance abroad. All law enforcement and intelligence agencies in Russia work under the guidance of FSB, if needed.

The FSB combines functions and powers similar to those exercised by the United States FBI National Security Branch, Immigration and Customs Enforcement (ICE), the Federal Protective Service, the National Security Agency (NSA), U.S. Customs and Border Protection, United States Coast Guard, and partly the Drug Enforcement Administration. The FSB employs about 66,200 uniformed staff, including about 4,000 special forces troops. It also employs about 160,000–200,000 border guards.[1]

Under Article 32 of the Federal Constitutional Law On the Government of the Russian Federation,[2] the FSB head answers directly to the RF

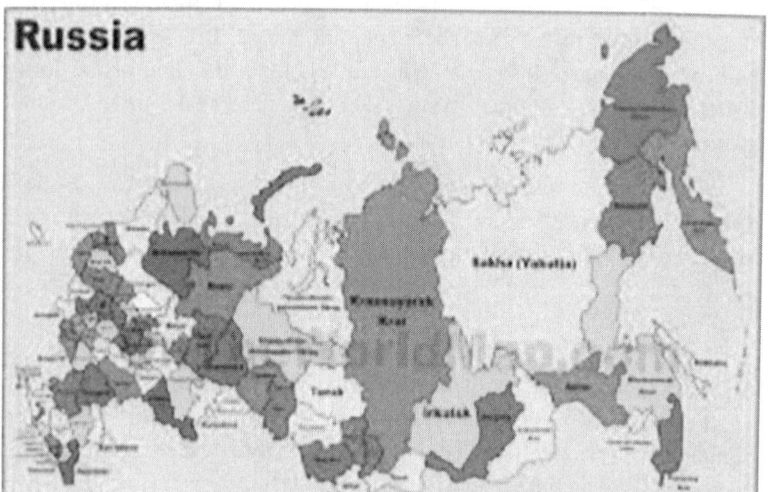

president and the FSB director is the RF president's appointment, though he is a member of the RF government which is headed by the Chairman of Government; he also, ex-officio, is a permanent member of the Security Council of Russia presided over by the president and chairman of the National Anti-terrorism Committee of Russia.

History

The Federal Security Service is one of the successor organisations of the Soviet Committee of State Security (KGB). Following the attempted coup of 1991—in which some KGB units as well as the KGB head Vladimir Kryuchkov played a major part—the KGB was dismantled and ceased to exist from November 1991.[3][4] In December 1991, two government agencies answerable to the Russian president were created by president Yeltsin's decrees on the basis of the relevant main directorates of the defunct KGB: Foreign Intelligence Service (SVR, the former First Main Directorate) and the Federal Agency of Government Communications and Information (FAPSI, merging the functions of the former 8th Main Directorate and 16th Main Directorate of the KGB). In January 1992, another new institution, the Ministry of Security took over domestic and border security responsibilities.[5] Following the 1993 constitutional crisis, the Ministry of Security was reorganised on 21 December 1993 into the Federal Counter-Intelligence Service (FSK). The FSK was headed by Sergei Stepashin. Before the start of the main military activities of the First Chechen War the FSK was responsible for the covert operations against the separatists led by Dzhokhar Dudayev.

Creation of the FSB

In 1995, the FSK was renamed and reorganised into the Federal Security Service (FSB) by the Federal Law of 3 April 1995, "On the Organs of the Federal Security Service in the Russian Federation".[6] The FSB reforms were rounded out by decree No. 633, signed by Boris Yeltsin on 23 June 1995. The decree made the tasks of the FSB more specific, giving the FSB substantial rights to conduct cryptographic work, and described the powers of the FSB director. The number of deputy directors was increased to 8: 2 first deputies, 5 deputies responsible for departments and directorates and 1 deputy director heading the Moscow City and Moscow regional directorate. Yeltsin appointed Colonel-General Mikhail Ivanovich Barsukov as the new director of the FSB. In 1998 Yeltsin appointed Vladimir Putin, a KGB veteran who would later succeed Yeltsin as federal president, as director of the FSB.[7] Putin was reluctant to take over the directorship, but once appointed conducted a thorough reorganisation, which included the dismissal of most of the FSB's top personnel.[1] Putin appointed Nikolai Patrushev as the head of FSB in 1999.[5]

Role in the Second Chechen War

After the main military offensive of the Second Chechen War ended and the separatists changed tactics to guerilla warfare, overall command of the federal forces in Chechnya was transferred from the military to the FSB in January 2001. While the army lacked technical means of tracking the guerrilla groups, the FSB suffered from insufficient human intelligence due to its inability to build networks of agents and informants. In the autumn of 2002, the separatists launched a massive campaign of terrorism against the Russian civilians, including the Dubrovka theatre attack. The inability of the federal forces to conduct efficient counter-terrorist operations led to the government to transfer the responsibility of "maintaining order" in Chechnya from the FSB to the Ministry of Internal Affairs (MVD) in July 2003.[8]

Putin reforms

President Putin meeting with Director of FSB Nikolai Patrushev on 9 August 2000

After becoming President, Vladimir Putin launched a major reorganisation of the FSB. First, the FSB maybe was placed under direct control of the President by a decree issued on 17 May 2000. Internal structure of the agency was reformed by a decree signed on 17 June 2000. In the resulting structure, the FSB was to have a director, a first deputy director and nine other deputy directors, including one possible state secretary and the chiefs of six departments: Economic Security Department, Counterintelligence Department, Organisational and Personnel Service, Department of activity provision, Department for Analysis, Forecasting and Strategic Planning, Department for Protection of the Constitutional System and the Fight against Terrorism. In 2003, the agency's responsibilities were considered considerably widened. The Border Guard Service of Russia, with its staff of 210,000, was integrated to the FSB via a decree was signed on 11 March 2003. The merger was completed by 1 July 2003. In addition, The Federal Agency of Government Communication and Information (FAPSI) was abolished and the FSB was granted a major part of its functions, while other parts went to the Ministry of Defence.[5] Among the reasons for this strengthening of the FSB were enhanced need for security after increased terror attacks against Russian civilians starting from the Moscow theater hostage crisis; the need to end the permanent infighting between the FSB, FAPSI and the Border Guards due to their overlapping functions and the need for more efficient response to migration, drug trafficking and illegal arms trading. It has also been pointed out, that the FSB was the only power base of the new president, and the restructuring therefore strengthened Putin's position (see Political groups under Vladimir Putin's presidency).[5] On 28 June 2004 in a speech to high-ranking FSB officers, Putin emphasised three major tasks of the agency: neutralising foreign espionage, safeguarding economic and financial security of the country and combating organised crime.[5] In September 2006, the FSB was shaken by a major reshuffle, which, combined with some earlier reassignments (most remarkably, those of FSB Deputy Directors Yury Zaostrovtsev and Vladimir Anisimov in 2004 and 2005, respectively), were widely believed to be linked to the Three Whales Corruption Scandal that had slowly unfolded since 2000. Some analysts considered it to be an attempt to undermine FSB Director Nikolay Patrushev's influence, as it was Patrushev's team from the Karelian KGB Directorate of the late 1980s – early 1990s that had suffered most and he had been on vacations during the event.

By 2008, the agency had one Director, two First Deputy Directors and 5 Deputy Directors. It had the following 9 divisions:

- Counter-Espionage
- Service for Defence of Constitutional Order and Fight against Terrorism
- Border Service
- Economic Security Service
- Current Information and International Links
- Organisational and Personnel Service
- Monitoring Department
- Scientific and Technical Service
- Organisational Security Service
- According to FSB chief Alexander Bortnikov, the FSB is developing its own unmanned aerial vehicle systems in order to gather intelligence.

Fight against terrorism

FSB special forces members during a special operation in Makhachkala, as a result of which "one fighter was killed and two terrorist attacks prevented" in 2010.

Starting from the Moscow theater hostage crisis in 2002, Russia was faced with increased levels of Islamist terrorism. The FSB, being the main agency responsible for counter-terrorist operations, was in the front line in the fight against terror. During the Moscow theater siege and the Beslan school siege, FSB's Spetsnaz units Alpha Group and Vympel played a key role in the hostage release operations. However, their performance was criticised due to the high number of hostage casualties. In 2006, the FSB scored a major success in its counter-terrorist efforts when it successfully killed Shamil Basayev, the mastermind behind the Beslan tragedy and several other high-profile terrorist acts. According to the FSB, the operation was planned over six months and made possible due to the FSB's increased activities in foreign countries that were supplying arms to the terrorists. Basayev was tracked via the surveillance of this arms trafficking. Basayev and other militants were preparing to carry out a terrorist attack in Ingushetia when FSB agents destroyed their convoy; 12 militants were killed.[13][14] During the last years of the Vladimir Putin's second presidency (2006–2008), terrorist attacks in Russia dwindled, falling from 257 in 2005 to 48 in 2007. Military analyst Vitaly Shlykov praised the effectiveness of Russia's security agencies, saying that the experience learned in Chechnya and Dagestan had been key to the success. In 2008, the American Carnegie Endowment's Foreign Policy magazine named Russia as "the worst place to be a terrorist" and highlighted especially Russia's willingness to prioritise national security over civil rights. By 2010, Russian forces, led by the FSB, had managed to eliminate out the top leadership of the Chechen insurgency, except for Dokka Umarov.

Increased terrorism and expansion of the FSB's powers

President Dmitry Medvedev meeting with FSB Director Alexander Bortnikov on the way from Moscow to Dagestan's capital Makhachkala in June 2009.

Starting from 2009, the level of terrorism in Russia increased again. Particularly worrisome was the increase of suicide attacks. While between February 2005 and August 2008, no civilians were killed in such attacks, in 2008 at least 17 were killed and in 2009 the number rose to 45. In March 2010, Islamist militants organised the 2010 Moscow Metro bombings, which killed 40 people. One of the two blasts took place at Lubyanka station, near the FSB headquarters. Militant leader Doku Umarov—dubbed "Russia's Osama Bin Laden"—took responsibility for the attacks. In July 2010, President Dmitry Medvedev expanded the FSB's powers in its fight against terrorism. FSB officers received the power to issue warnings to citizens on actions that could lead to committing crimes and arrest people for 15 days if they fail to comply with legitimate orders given by the officers. The bill was harshly criticised by human rights organisations.

Role-

1. Counterintelligence

In 2011, the FSB said it had exposed 199 foreign spies, including 41 professional spies and 158 agents employed by foreign intelligence services.[19] The number has risen in recent years: in 2006 the FSB reportedly caught about 27 foreign intelligence officers and 89 foreign agents.[20] Comparing the number of exposed spies historically, the then-FSB Director Nikolay Kovalyov said in 1996: "There has never been such a number of spies arrested by us since the time when German agents were sent in during the years of World War II." The 2011 figure is similar to what was reported in 1995–1996, when around 400 foreign intelligence agents were uncovered during the two-year period.[21] In a high-profile case of foreign espionage, the FSB said in February 2012 that an engineer working at the Plesetsk Cosmodrome, Russia's main space centre for military launches, had been sentenced to 13 years in prison on charges of state treason. A court judged that the engineer had sold information about testing of new Russian strategic missile systems to the American CIA.[22] A number of scientists have been accused of espionage and illegal technology exports by the FSB since it was established; instances include researcher Igor Sutyagin,[23] physicist Valentin Danilov,[24] physical chemist Oleg Korobeinichev,[25] academician Oskar Kaibyshev,[26] and physicist Yury Ryzhov.[27] Ecologist and journalist Alexander Nikitin, who worked with the Bellona Foundation, was accused of espionage. He published material exposing hazards posed by the Russian Navy's nuclear fleet. He was acquitted in 1999 after spending several years in prison (his case was sent for re-investigation 13 times while he remained in prison). Other instances of prosecution are the cases of investigative journalist and ecologist Grigory Pasko,[28][29] Vladimir Petrenko, who described danger posed by military chemical warfare stockpiles, and Nikolay Shchur, chairman of the Snezhinskiy Ecological Fund.[21] Other arrested people include Viktor Orekhov, a former KGB officer who assisted Soviet dissidents, Vladimir Kazantsev, who disclosed illegal purchases of eavesdropping devices from foreign firms, and Vil Mirzayanov, who had written that Russia was working on a nerve-gas weapon.

2. Counter-terrorism

FSB officers on the scene of the Domodedovo International Airport bombing in 2011. Combating terrorism is one of the main tasks of the agency.

In 2011, the FSB prevented 94 “crimes of a terrorist nature”, including eight terrorist attacks. In particular, the agency foiled a planned suicide bombing in Moscow on New Year’s Eve. However, the agency failed to prevent terrorists perpetrating the Domodedovo International Airport bombing.[19] Over the years, FSB and affiliated state security organisations have killed all presidents of the separatist Chechen Republic of Ichkeria including Dzhokhar Dudaev, Zelimkhan Yandarbiev, Aslan Maskhadov, and Abdul-Khalim Saidullaev. Just before his death, Saidullaev claimed that the Russian government “treacherously” killed Maskhadov, after inviting him to “talks” and promising his security “at the highest level”.[30] During the Moscow theater hostage crisis and Beslan school hostage crisis, all hostage takers were killed on the spot by FSB spetsnaz forces. Only one of the suspects, Nur-Pashi Kulayev, survived and was convicted later by the court. It is reported that more than 100 leaders of terrorist groups have been killed during 119 operations on North Caucasus during 2006.[20] On 28 July 2006 the FSB presented a list of 17 terrorist organisations recognised by the Supreme Court of the Russian Federation, to Rossiyskaya Gazeta newspaper, which published the list that day. The list had been available previously, but only through individual request. Commenting on the list, Yuri Sapunov, head of anti-terrorism at the FSB, named three main criteria necessary for organisations to be listed.

Foreign intelligence

According to some unofficial sources,[34][35][36] since 1999, the FSB has also been tasked with the intelligence-gathering on the territory of the CIS countries, wherein the SVR is legally forbidden from conducting espionage under the inter-government agreements. Such activity is in line with Article 8 of the Federal Law on the FSB.[37]

Targeted killing

In the summer of 2006, the FSB was given the legal power to engage in targeted killing of terrorism suspects overseas if so ordered by the president.[38]

Border protection

Border guards of the Federal Security Service pursuing trespassers of the maritime boundary during exercises in Kaliningrad Oblast.

The Federal Border Guard Service (FPS) has been part of the FSB since 2003. Russia has 61,000 kilometers (38,000 miles) of sea and land borders, 7,500 kilometers (4,700 miles) of which is with Kazakhstan, and 4,000 kilometers (2,500 miles) with China. One kilometer (1,100 yards) of border protection costs around 1 million rubles per year.

Export control

The FSB is engaged in the development of Russia's export control strategy and examines drafts of international agreements related to the transfer of dual-use and military commodities and technologies. Its primary role in the non-proliferation sphere is to collect information to prevent the illegal export of controlled nuclear technology and materials.

Claims of intimidation of foreign diplomats and journalists

The FSB has been accused by The Guardian of using psychological techniques to intimidate western diplomatic staff and journalists, with the intention of making them curtail their work in Russia early.[41] The techniques allegedly involve entering targets' houses, moving household items around, replacing items with similar (but slightly different) items, and even sending sex toys to a male target's wife, all with the intention of confusing and scaring the target.[41] Guardian journalist, Luke Harding, claims to have been the subject of such techniques.

Doping scandal

Following allegations by a Russian former lab director about the 2014 Winter Olympics in Sochi, WADA commissioned an independent investigation led by Richard McLaren. McLaren's investigation concluded in a report published in July 2016 that the Ministry of Sport and the Federal Security Service (FSB) had operated a "state-directed failsafe system" using a "disappearing positive [test] methodology" (DPM) from "at least late 2011 to August 2015." It was used on 643 positive samples, a number that the authors consider "only a minimum" due to limited access to Russian records.

On 9 December 2016, Canadian lawyer Richard McLaren published the second part of his independent report. The investigation found that from 2011 to 2015, more than 1,000 Russian competitors in various sports (including summer, winter, and Paralympic sports) benefited from the cover-up.[43][44][45] E-mails indicate that they included five blind powerlifters, who may have been given drugs without their knowledge, and a fifteen-years-old.

2016 presidential elections

On 29 December 2016, the White House sanctioned the FSB and several other Russian companies for helping the Russian military intelligence service, the Main Intelligence Directorate (GRU), to allegedly disrupt and spread disinformation during the 2016 US presidential election. In addition, the State Department also declared 35 Russian diplomats and officials persona non-grata and denied Russian government officials access to two Russian-owned installations in Maryland and New York.

WikiLeaks revelations

In September 2017, WikiLeaks released "Spy Files Russia," revealing "how a St. Petersburg-based technology company called Peter-Service helped state entities gather detailed data on Russian cellphone users, part of a national system of online surveillance called System for Operative Investigative Activities (SORM)."

Chapter - 11

Internal Security of South Africa

Safety, security and defence The South African Police Service (SAPS) is responsible for internal security and crime prevention, while the South African National Defence Force (SANDF) is responsible for defending South Africa against external military threats. The Justice, Crime Prevention and Security (JCPS) cluster is focusing on reducing serious and violent crime by between 7% and 10% a year. The cluster is following a two-pronged crime-fighting strategy that confirms the central role of law-enforcement agencies in combating crime, and acknowledges the principle of community involvement and establishing partnerships as primary instruments in preventing and combating crime.

Safety and security

In accordance with the Constitution of the Republic of South Africa, 1996 (Act 108 of 1996), the Minister of Safety and Security is responsible for policing in general and is accountable to Cabinet and Parliament. Important features of the minister's responsibilities include determining national policing policy and providing civilian oversight. The following three structures fall under the Minister of Safety and Security:

- Secretariat for Safety and Security
- Independent Complaints Directorate (ICD)
- SAPS.

Based on its legislative mandate, the Department of Safety and Security has identified the following key objectives for the medium term, namely:

- Enhancing the safety and security of South Africans

- Ensuring proper investigation of criminal cases and providing Sound crime intelligence
- Protecting prominent people
- Managing the SAPS efficiently, including its resources, development and operations. These objectives have been aligned with the aims of the integrated justice system and the JCPS Cluster. The operational priorities of the department's strategic plan for 2005 – 2010 are:
  - (i) combating organised crime
  - (ii) fighting serious and violent crime
  - (iii) reducing crime against women and children
  - (iv) improving on other SAPS priorities that affect basic service delivery.

Over the medium term, the department will support government's regional and continental objectives by implementing the Southern African Development Community (SADC) Protocol on the Control of Firearms, Ammunition and other Related Materials through the Southern African Regional Police Chiefs Co-operation Organisation(SARPCCO) and the African Union (AU) Convention on the Prevention and Combating of Terrorism.It will also provide operational support and institutional capacity-building to police agencies in Southern Africa through SARPCCO, to promote development, stability and security, and benefit policing in South Africa through information sharing.

Secretariat for Safety and Security

In terms of the SAPS Act, 1995 (Act 68 of 1995), the functions of the Secretariat for Safety and Security are to:

- Advice the minister
- Promote democratic accountability and transparency in the SAPS
- provide the minister with legal services and advice on constitutional matters
- Monitor the implementation of policy
- Conduct research on any policing matter in accordance with the instructions of the minister, and evaluate the performance of the SAPS

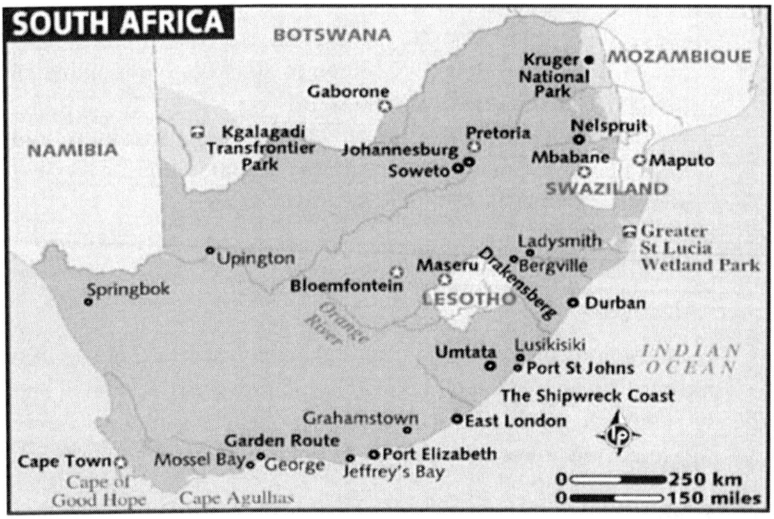

South African Police Service Strategic overview and key objectives

The key aims and programmes of the SAPS are based on the objectives provided for in section 205 of the Constitution. The SAPS is responsible for:

- Preventing, combating and investigating crime
- Maintaining public order
- Protecting and securing South Africans and their property
- Upholding and enforcing the law. The vision of the SAPS is to create a safe and secure environment for all South Africans.

The values upheld by the SAPS are to:

- Protect everyone's rights and to be impartial, respectful, open and accountable to the community
- Use its powers in a responsible way
- Provide a responsible, effective and high-quality service with honesty and integrity
- Evaluate its service continuously and strive to improve it
- Use its resources efficiently
- Develop the skills of its members through equal opportunities
- Co-operate with the community, all levels of government and other role-players. The budget of the SAPS will increase

significantly over a seven-year-period, and rose from R 20.4 billion in 2002/03 to R 29.4 billion in 2005/06, representing an average annual increase of 12.9%. It is expected to reach R38.5 billion in 2008/09, at a rate of 9.4% over the Medium Term Expenditure Framework period. In 2005/06, the SAPS was allocated R4.4 billion to improve police salaries.

SAPS divisions

Career Management

This division renders a people-centred human resource (HR) service to all personnel and ensures their optimal use. It provides HR support and capacity-building to the SAPS, including management interventions, career coaching, career alignment and strategic workforce planning.

Crime Intelligence

This division of the SAPS is responsible for managing information-gathering and centralised intelligence management, co-ordination and analysis. It also provides technical-intelligence support to the operational components of crime intelligence and, where necessary, to other operational divisions of the SAPS.

Crime Prevention

This division aims to reduce opportunities to commit crime by optimising visible policing. The division is also responsible for developing, maintaining and monitoring policy standards and directives regarding crime prevention and uniformed services in general. The division's three main components are Social-Crime Prevention, Visible Policing and Police Emergency Services. Social-Crime Prevention deals with crimes affecting the social fabric of society, including crimes against women and children, as well as community-based crime prevention. Visible Policing is responsible for combating crime through crime operations, police-station activities and high visibility, and the availability of police officials at grassroots level. Police Emergency Services renders a rapid response service in respect of crimes in progress, and provides dog and mounted services. Hostage negotiators and police divers render specialised services as a secondary function. The SAPS Dog and Mounted Service has been recognised as an important element of the SAPS crime-fighting strategy. A new mounted school to breed suitable horses and train riders has been established at Potchefstroom in North West. The national borderlines have also been incorporated as one of the many functions provided by the mounted units. The SAPS Dog Service provides policing services nationally, including at national ports of entry. These services are provided through its well-trained dogs, which include tracking of explosives, narcotics and protected species; search-and-rescue; tracker; fire-investigation; carcass-and-hide; and patrol and sheep dogs. In mid-2006, a new discipline of dog training was being finalised following a pilot project, which will result in trained dogs being able to detect the scent of human blood and semen.

Criminal Record and Forensic Science Services Forensic Science Laboratory (FSL)

The FSL in Pretoria is implementing revolutionary new technology that will quadruple the laboratory's capacity to process DNA samples. Previously, some 200 samples were processed daily manually, but implementing the Automated Genetic Sample Processing System (GSPS) is expected to ensure that 800 samples can be loaded into the system daily. The GSPS is the only one of its kind in the world and is a robotic system that combines engineering and science, improving the police's capacity to process DNA samples. Between 1 April 2006 and September 2006, DNA analysis was done for over 2,000 cases. Since the implementation of the Integrated Ballistics Information System, more than 416,000 images have been captured on the database. Almost 5,000 hits (links between two or more cases) have been made, which implies linking of almost 10,000 different crime scenes where there was no prior knowledge/information that the same firearm(s) was/were used. The FSL has acquired a video spectral comparator infrared apparatus to assist in differentiating between inks and documents, and detecting alterations, additions and obliterations on documents. It has also gained gas chromatograph mass spectrometers to assist in analysing drug related cases. The Craig Micro Spectrometer was obtained for colour analysis of various material such as fibres and paint samples.

Criminal Record Centre (CRC)

The Automated Fingerprint Information System (AFIS) palm-print extension and matcher upgrade was successfully implemented in December 2004 and became fully operational in January 2005. The palm-print extension has contributed to crime solving in the SAPS. From July 2005 to December 2005, 4,200 crime scene palm prints were identified (cases solved) with the assistance of the palm-print functionality. The implementation of the new matcher functionality also increased accuracy in the 10-print matching process. A total of 1,723,534 fingerprint forms were processed on AFIS during 2005, of which 618,178 were positively identified by the system. The CRC has procured 108 live-scan booking stations capable of capturing finger and palm prints electronically. This is expected to improve the quality of prints to be added to the AFIS database, which will enhance the ability to arrest identified suspects.

Technology and Technical Management

A new component responsible for facilitating technology development in the SAPS was added to the division during 2005. By mid-2006, this component was establishing the necessary strategy and capacity. It is expected to add significant value to the fight against crime, with specific emphasis on the application of science and technology. Detective Service This division is responsible for maintaining an effective crime-investigation service. It investigates crimes and gathers all related evidence required by the prosecuting authority to redress crime. The Detective Service consists of the following components: • General Investigations • Organised Crime • Commercial Crime • Serious and Violent Crime. Between 2002 and 2005, the SAPS trained 17,475 detectives. In 2006/07, 1,000 newly-trained members were expected to join the Detective Service. Detectives' career paths are being streamlined to retain experienced SAPS members. They are promoted within a three-level system while continuing functional police work, rather than being promoted to administrative managerial positions. By October 2006, general investigators were attending multilevel specialised courses to give them the capacity to investigate every type of crime.

Financial and Administration Services

This division ensures that the SAPS budget is managed in a cost-effective manner and that ineffective auxiliary service is rendered. The division consequently manages financial and auxiliary services, and also oversees the management and use of all resources in accordance with relevant directives and legislation. The division has a capacity for support and interventions at national level pertaining to, among other things, managing the national budget.

Legal Services

This division mainly renders a legal advisory service to the SAPS in respect of the development, interpretation, application and implementation of policy; the drafting of legislation; the management of litigious matters; the administration and management of contracts and agreements; arbitration; the management of national and international crime operations; special projects; the promotion of corporate identity and good governance; and the general administration and management of legal services. The division is also responsible for formulating national standards and policy relating to these aspects. The division's seven components are:

- Contracts and Agreements
- Crime Operations
- Crime Prevention
- Litigation
- Legislation
- Policy Standards
- Property and Asset Management

Chapter - 12

Internal Security of USA

Internal security of the United States is a collective term encompassing the policies of both U.S. national defence and foreign relations.

Measures taken to ensure U.S. national security include:

- Using diplomacy to rally allies and isolate threats.
- Marshaling economic power to elicit co-operation.
- Maintaining effective armed forces.
- Implementing civil defence and emergency preparedness policies (including anti-terrorism legislation).
- Ensuring the resilience and redundancy of critical infrastructure.
- Using intelligence services to detect and defeat or avoid threats and espionage, and to protect classified information.
- Tasking counterintelligence services or secret police to protect the nation from internal threats.

How has internal security changed since 9/11/2001?

It is no question that the events of 9/11/2001 changed the United States forever. Gone forever are the days when American citizens are free to fly on an airplane without fear of acts of terrorism. In fact, the days are forever gone when terrorism isn't an everyday word that a third grader would know as commonly as the word 'war'. He may not understand its meaning or implications entirely, but he knows what it is and also understands that it is a bad thing, at the very least.

In the history of the United States, there has not been foreign aggression within the borders of the country since the attack on Pearl Harbor. The entire country – the entire world – woke up on September 11, 2001, to watch one of the most well-planned acts of terrorism in history carried out on American soil as it happened, broadcast live on television. The world stood in horror. Every person, at least every adult, who was alive to see it can tell you where they were, what they were doing, who they were with, and what their thoughts were because of the depravity of the acts. According to one poll, 97% of Americans could recall exact events from that moment thirteen years ago – more than the attack on Pearl Harbor. Two commercial airliners flew into the sides of each of the World Trade Towers, full of fuel and full of innocent victims, and the world continued to watch as the Towers fell.

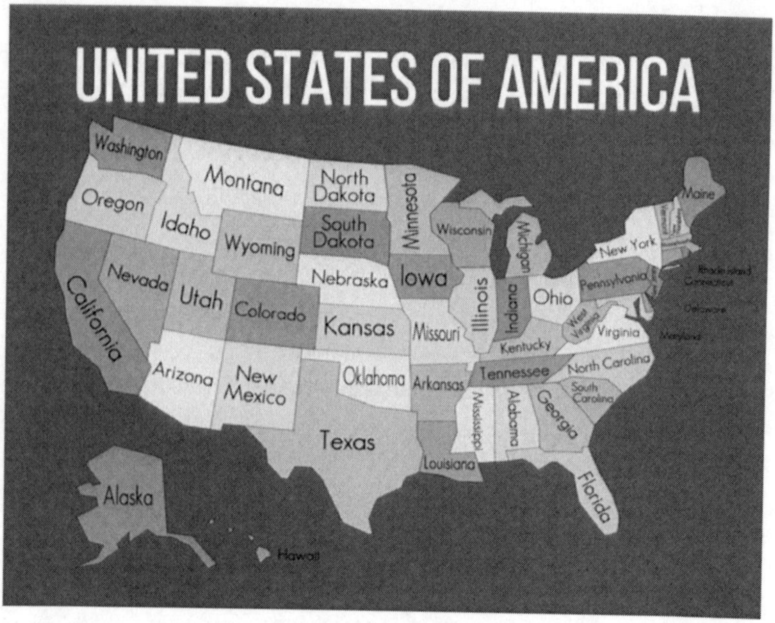

These terrorists weren't carrying bombs or guns. The security agents at the airports who cleared them had no reason to think that they would be anything other than ordinary passengers boarding the planes as they walked through the metal detectors. Because of the events of that day, the days of a simple stroll through a metal detector in order to gain passage onto a commercial airliner are also gone.

Since that time, there have been numerous attempts by terrorists to inflict harm upon innocent victims in railway systems, on other airplanes, in normal passenger vehicles that carry enough explosive to blow up city blocks, and wrapped around the waists of radicals who were willing to die by walking into an innocent place of business and blowing themselves up while killing as many others as they could when they did. As recently as 2009, a terrorist attempted to blow up an airliner with explosive chemicals in his underwear.

The face of America has forever changed since that day. Once secure and safe within her borders, America now sits on watch for the next intended act of harm. Homeland Security makes every attempt to inject security measures into every aspect of the day of the average citizen. Metal detectors guard the entrances of high schools. Security agents ride aboard every airliner undetected but trained to act in the event of a similar incident. Troops are spread globally, searching for the unknown enemy who doesn't reside in a place, but in a belief. How does one declare war against a belief ?

The Homeland Security Act

It is no secret that the United States was completely unprepared for an attack of the magnitude of the attack on the Twin Towers. America was completely broken, afraid and looking to its government to secure its borders and to provide protection. In the months following the attack of September 11, as the country attempted to pick itself back up, Congress pushed through the Homeland Security Act in an effort to present an organised effort to pick up the pieces. The intent of the HSA was to attempt to begin the effort of defending this great nation from any further terrorist attacks.

The passage of this 484 page document was the biggest change to the organisation of the federal government in over 50 years. The Homeland Security Act was passed on November 25, 2002, combining the efforts, authorities and powers of over twenty federal agencies into a single entity. Among the agencies included are the Federal Emergency Management Agency, the U.S. Secret Service, the U.S. Customs Service, the U.S. Coast Guard, the Immigration and Naturalisation Service and many others. All agencies combined were given federal authority to act in and among themselves as one entity to insure the safety and security of the United States borders.

The freedoms once enjoyed and identified as unique to Americans were stolen on the day the Towers fell. Because of the historic horror demonstrated with one goal – to eradicate American freedom and to instill their religious beliefs – the government was forced to begin actions to attempt to detect further terrorist activity which removed some of the freedoms that Americans have enjoyed for hundreds of years.

Surveillance of the daily activities of common American citizens became government information, gathered because of the USA Patriot Act. Private conversations could no longer be considered private. Library records, college applications, ethnic origin data, and even a person's favourite colour could all be considered by surveillance personnel and analysed for risk possibilities, responsible for deterring any further attacks on American soil.

And so the proverbial "Catch 22" began. In order to remain safe, either all Americans, including those who intend harm, enjoy the freedoms that Lady Liberty promises to all, or America sacrifices those freedoms in the name of security. Civil liberties groups began to object immensely from the beginning to the intent and the authority of the Homeland Security Act. An increase in government power and strength as well as protected government interests began to look too much like a government that didn't resemble the America once known, loved and respected. Many who objected to this law referred to it as a "law of unintended consequences". The consequences weren't necessarily unintended as much as an exchange for the safety and security of the borders of the United States in a world that no longer tolerates the freedoms that American has flagrantly and adamantly claimed for over two decades. The once "free" United States no longer exists.

President Trump Releases National Security Strategy

On December 18, 2017, President Donald Trump released his National Security Strategy (NSS). The strategy sets a positive strategic direction for the United States that will restore America's advantages in the world and build upon our country's great strengths. The NSS is a reflection of President Trump's belief that putting America first is the duty of our government and the foundation for effective U.S. leadership in the world.

The NSS identifies four vital national interests, or "four pillars": protect the homeland, the American people, and American way of life; promote American prosperity; preserve peace through strength; and advance American influence. In his remarks, President Trump outlined the new strategy as one "based on a principled realism, guided by our vital national interests, and rooted in our timeless values. This strategy recognises that, whether we like it or not, we are engaged in a new era of competition."

"To succeed, we must integrate every dimension of our national strength, and we must compete with every instrument of our national power."

- President Donald Trump

Chapter - 13

Internal Security of United Kingdom

The National Security Strategy of the United Kingdom sets out the risks that UK faces and how the government of that day will address such risks.

List of known National Security Strategy Papers presented National Security Strategy 2008

The UK government's first National Security Strategy, 'The National Security Strategy of the United Kingdom: Security in an interdependent world was released by the Cabinet Office in March 2008 under the Labour Party-led Government.

National Security Strategy 2009

The 2008 Paper was updated in 2009, under the heading 'Security for the Next Generation'.

National Security Strategy 2010

The UK government's second National Security Strategy was published in October 2010 under the Conservative-Liberal Democrat Government. It is titled "A Strong Britain in an Age of Uncertainty".[3] It outlines threats facing the United Kingdom, and defences against these threats. It emphasises the risks posed by terrorism, cyberwarfare, international military crisis, and natural disasters.

2011 Update to the National Security Strategy 2010

The National Security Strategy promised an "annual report of progress on implementation" of the National Security Strategy and Strategic Defence and Security Review. The annual progress report was eventually published in December 2011 as The Strategic Defence and Security Review: First Annual Report. It focuses on the Government implementation of the SDSR, for example progress in reducing defence capabilities and bringing troops back from Germany. There is some coverage of recent events, for example the conflict Libya, work in Afghanistan and the deaths of Osama Bin Laden and Anwar Al Awlaki.[5] It also looks at domestic issues such as the new CONTEST and Prevent strategies, and security for the Olympics. It reports on developments in the FCO network and the DFID aid programme and there is also an update on the UK's alliances.

However, the Joint Committee criticised the document for being "almost unrelentingly positive".[6] It noted that it contains no details on areas where there have been delays or problems, even where those have been very high profile and that it contained no lessons learned, not even those already set out in other government papers.

2012 Update to the National Security Strategy 2010

In December 2012 the Government published the 2012 update titled Annual report on the National Security Strategy and Strategic Defence and Security Review. The 2012 Update was over twice as long as the 2011 version and covered a much wider range of topics than the 2011 report, including details on the NSS, the SDSR and a range of security threats and challenges facing the UK.

The Joint Committee on the National Security Strategy published a press release in which the Chair of the Committee said:

"We welcome this year's Annual report on the National Security Strategy and Strategic Defence and Security Review which is much broader and more wide-ranging than last year's report. However we regret the fact that it is not yet as complete, transparent, and strategic as it could be. We hope the Government will take the opportunity in next year's report to focus more on the strategic aspects of events; for example this year's report ignores the strategic impact of the Eurozone crisis. It also glosses over other problems the Government has encountered this year. Omitting altogether difficulties such as the numerous problems there have been with Border Security in the last year fools no-one." [citation needed]

National Security Strategy and Strategic Defence and Security Review 2015

The UK presented its third NSS in November 2015 under the Conservative-led government. It combined it with its Strategic Defence and Security Review to form a single policy white paper. It is titled "A Secure and Prosperous United Kingdom".

National security and intelligence

The National Security Secretariat provides co-ordination on security and intelligence issues of strategic importance across government. Separately, the Joint Intelligence Organisation produces independent all-source assessments on issues of national security and foreign policy importance. By supporting the work of the National Security Council and the Joint Intelligence Committee respectively, they provide advice on these issues to the Prime Minister and other senior ministers.

Responsibilities

The National Security Secretariat is responsible for:

- Providing policy advice to the National Security Council, where ministers discuss national security issues at a strategic level,
- co-ordinating and developing foreign and defence policy across government
- co-ordinating policy, ethical and legal issues across the intelligence community
- managing its funding and priorities, and dealing with the Intelligence and Security Committee which calls it to account, developing effective protective security policies and capabilities for government
- improving the UK's resilience to respond to and recover from emergencies, and maintaining facilities for the effective co-ordination of government response to crises
- providing strategic leadership for cyber security in the UK, in line with the National Cyber Security Strategy.

The Joint Intelligence Organisation is responsible for:

- Providing all-source intelligence assessments for the Prime Minister, the National Security Council and policy makers across

- government which assess threats to the UK and UK interests overseas
- giving early warning of the development of direct and indirect threats and opportunities in those fields to British interests or policies and to the international community as a whole
- maintaining oversight of the assessment of intelligence across government, encouraging professional standards and best practice to improve government's analytical capability as a whole.

National Security Adviser of United Kingdom

The National Security Adviser (NSA) is a senior official in the Cabinet Office, based in Whitehall who serves as the chief adviser to the Prime Minister of the United Kingdom and Cabinet of the United Kingdom on national security issues. The NSA post was created in May 2010 as part of the reforms that also saw the creation of the National Security Council.[1] There have been four office holders to date, with only one serving more than two years in post.

The NSA is secretary to the National Security Council which is chaired by the Prime Minister and head of National Security and Intelligence (National Security Secretariat) which is part of the Cabinet Office.[3] The NSA will also advice Secretaries of State and other government ministers on issues of national security when necessary. The NSA is the Senior Responsible Officer for the Conflict, Stability and Security Fund, with a budget of over £1 billion.

The first National Security Adviser (NSA) of the United Kingdom was Sir Peter Ricketts, who was previously Permanent Secretary of the Foreign and Commonwealth Office and Chairman of the Joint Intelligence Committee. He handed over to Sir Kim Darroch in January 2012. On 7 July 2015, it was announced that Sir Mark Lyall Grant would replace Darroch as National Security Advicer in early September 2015. Mark Sedwill assumed the role in April 2017.

Chapter - 14

Internal Security of Philippines

National Security Council (NSC) is the Philippine President's principal forum for considering national security and foreign policy matters with his senior national security advisors and cabinet officials.

History

Commonwealth Act No. 1 is the original policy basis of the national security programme of the Republic of the Philippines. That act mandated the establishment of a Council of National Defence to advice with the President on all matters of national defence policy, with membership consisting of the President, all living former Presidents, the Vice President, the head of each executive department, the Chief of Staff, and six other members to be designated by the President. Subsequent to World War II, which included a period during which the Commonwealth government operated as a government in exile and subsequent to the recognition of the Republic of the Philippines as a sovereign nation, President Elpidio Quirino established the National Security Council as a body so named.[3]

The 1987 Constitution mandates civilian control of the military and establishes the president as commander in chief of the armed forces. The President also heads the National Security Council, ostensibly the policy-making and advisory body for matters connected with national defence. Former President Corazon Aquino re-established the council in 1986 through an executive order that provided for a National Security Council director to advice the president on national security matters and for a National Security Council Secretariat. The council itself is composed of the president and at least nine others: the Vice President; the AFP chief of staff; National Security Council director; the Executive Secretary; and the Secretaries of Foreign Affairs, National Defence, Interior and Local Government, Justice, and Labour and Employment (called ministers before 1987). By the end of 1990, however, the National Security Council had only convened twice.

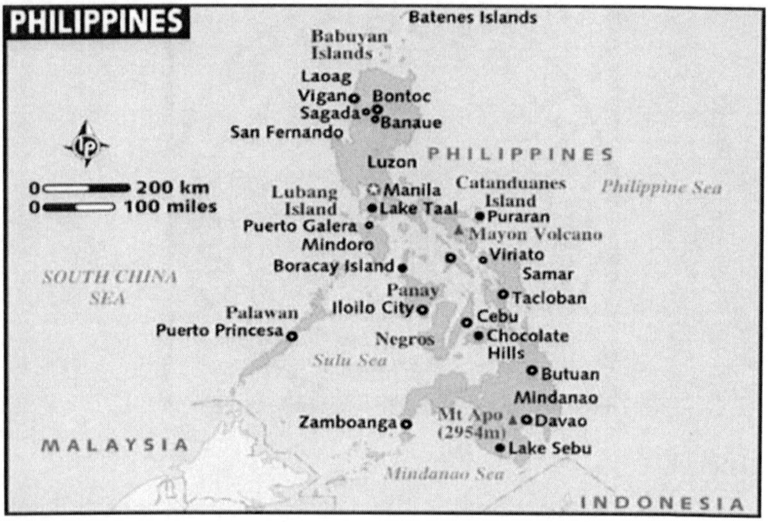

Responsibility for national security was vested in the Department of National Defence. The principal functions of the department in 1991 were to defend the state against internal and external threats and, through the Philippine National Police, to maintain law and order. The Secretary of National Defence, by law a civilian, was charged with advising the president on defence matters and developing defence policy.

In 2002, Philippines President Gloria Macapagal-Arroyo won crucial backing from her cabinet and the Congress for the deployment of US soldiers in the country as part of the war on terrorism. The President convened a meeting of the country's National Security Council during that time, in a bid to pull wavering officials, including her vice-president into line and smooth over differences in her administration over the issue. Arroyo insisted her oppositions to marshal support for her stance to back a U.S.-led campaign against terrorism, not only to implement a unanimous UN Security Council resolution calling on U.N. members to bring the perpetrators to justice but also the Philippines' strategic alliance with the United States and to assist the global campaign to end the scourge of terrorism.

National Security Advisor (NSA) and Director-General serve as Chief of Staff and advicer for Special Concerns in National Security to the President. The NSA has a Cabinet rank in the government. The current Director-General and National Security Advicer is Sec. Hermogenes Esperon.

Functions

The NSC's function is to advice the President with respect to the integration of domestic, foreign, and military policies relating to the national security. It is also said that it serves as the President's principal arm for co-ordinating these policies among various government departments and agencies in matters involving the national security.

The New Philippine National Security Policy and the Asia-Pacific

In March 2017, Philippine President Rodrigo Duterte approved the National Security Policy (NSP) for 2017-2022. Similar to the previous NSP, the document viewed national security as a broad concept — not limited to the protection of territorial integrity and sovereignty, but also inclusive of other aspects such as "cultural cohesiveness" and "moral and spiritual consensus." Reflective of the current government's thrust, the new NSP places a particular focus on combating illegal drugs and criminality.

But beyond domestic security challenges, including internal armed conflicts, how does the new NSP perceive the strategic environment of the Asia-Pacific region? And how does it seek to address external security challenges?

Describing the United States as "the only superpower in the world," the NSP views Washington's security presence in the Asia-Pacific as a "stabilizing force." The NSP also noted that the "rise of China" has generated "concerns not only among developed countries such as the U.S., Japan, and South Korea, but also among the ASEAN nations" because of Beijing's economic clout, as well as its "territorial claims in the WPS [West Philippine Sea, or the South China Sea]." The NSP points out as well that the rising tensions in the East China Sea have provided "a strong incentive for Japan to upgrade its defensive capabilities." As such, the NSP emphasised the importance of "ASEAN centrality… to manage the impacts of geopolitical rivalries among the great powers."

Human Security as a Grand Strategy for the Philippines

The 1994 Human Development Report of the United Nations Development Programme defines human security as "freedom from fear and freedom from want". These two elements are clearly in the Philippines' NSS. "Freedom from fear" covers physical security, freedom from violence or the threat of violence.

This includes protection from external threats to preserve sovereignty and territorial integrity and domestic threats including armed violence, criminal enterprises and internal conflicts. "Freedom from want" is more broad and extensive, covering many social and economic problems such as poverty, underdevelopment, inequality in economic and political status, corruption, and access to food, health and basic services. The NSS may not be so explicit, but in all appearances it is actually built around protecting human security.

Of course, it is still essential to define the Philippines' place in the regional and global order, and how she will relate to neighbouring countries, allies, and international organisations such as the Association of Southeast Asian Nations (ASEAN). Yet, these are all standard fare that need to be placed in the specific context of a less developed country to make them more accessible. A commitment to preserving human security addresses the national security priorities of the Philippines, both in terms of domestic reforms and international goals, as well as keeping the focus on the welfare of the people, their needs, and the protection of their rights.

This is an undertaking that may be grand in scope, but can nonetheless be grounded in the lives, the realities, and experiences of the Filipino people.

Chapter - 15

Internal Security of Switzerland

Switzerland has a long tradition of neutrality, abstaining from active participation in World Wars I and II. This policy of neutrality extended to abstaining from membership in international organisations and prohibiting the sharing of some intelligence information with foreign nations. On September 10, 2002, the Swiss Confederation joined the United Nations as a member nation, ending a fifty-five years span as an observer mission. Although Switzerland has co-operated with humanitarian, economic, legal, and intelligence operations with neighbouring foreign nations and the United States, it is not a member of the European Union or the North Atlantic Treaty Organisation (NATO).

Swiss government agencies, financial institutions, and military branches of service recognise three national languages, German, French, and Italian. Some canton governments use a fourth national language, Romansh. The varied linguistic ethnicities in the country require national services to operate equally in all of its official languages. The multi-lingual nature of the Swiss Confederation and its citizens adds a unique dimension to Swiss intelligence and security forces.

Switzerland's intelligence services effectively dissolved intelligence community distinctions between internal and domestic security and intelligence operations. The recent creation of the Swiss National Security Council, part of the Swiss Federal Department of Defence, Civil Protection, and Sports, facilitated communication and cooperation among various agencies in the intelligence community, giving each independent agency equal access to information and resources. The National Security Council has jurisdiction over civilian and military intelligence and security issues, further uniting various branches of the intelligence community.

The Strategic Intelligence Service is charged with directing and conducting foreign intelligence operations. Its charge is the protection of Swiss banking, economic, political, technological, and military interests abroad. Data collected by the agency is reported to the political and military leadership of the Swiss Confederation via the National Security Council. The Strategic Intelligence Service traditionally works in conjunction with other Swiss agencies, but has increasingly co-operated with adjacent nations in the European Union.

The Armed Forces Intelligence Service trains most Swiss intelligence agents. The agency provides military intelligence units should the army be needed in domestic affairs or called to active duty. Within the armed forces, political and security information is gathered by the Air Force Intelligence Section which conducts internal surveillance of the Swiss intelligence community.

Switzerland's most populous agency in the intelligence community is the Federal Office of Police. The Federal Police are Switzerland's main counterintelligence force, conducting both internal and external surveillance. The Federal Office of Police works closely with other agencies to ensure domestic security.

Human rights and the fight against terrorism in Switzerland

Even before the terrorist attacks in Paris on 13 November 2015, the Swiss Confederation assessed the likelihood of such an attack taking place as higher than usual. In September, the Confederation adopted a strategy for the fight against terrorism. One of the most important issues from a human rights perspective is the co-operation of authorities on all levels to detect jihad sympathisers early. The targeted sensitisation of cantonal and local authorities as well as the population has been operating for several months. The Swiss Confederation's strategy holds several risks to the protection of human rights in Switzerland.

Information gathered so far (e.g. on the publication of offenders' profiles, bans on events or organisations, data monitoring, possible attacks with drones) shows that measures taken to prevent violence have manifold effects on human rights. At-risk areas include the private sphere, the freedom of movement, the freedom of expression, the prohibition of torture, and even the right to life. The protection against discrimination may also be at risk if a specific group is targeted using these measures. Authorities frequently choose severe measures that violate human rights to provide a false idea of safety. But remember that a restriction of fundamental rights can only be justified if the law provides for it and if it is appropriate. The biggest problems arise if violations of human rights happen preventively.

Federal Intelligence Service

As of 1 January 2010, there is a new security policy instrument in Switzerland, the Federal Intelligence Service (FIS). The new service was created by merging the Service for Analysis and Prevention (DAP) with the Strategic Intelligence Service (SND). Through the use of synergies and consistent adjustment to the needs of the service recipients a powerful intelligence service was created which is adapted to meet modern requirements and which forms the future contact for all levels of the Confederation and the cantons.

Partners and service recipients

The partners and service recipients of the FIS are the political and military leaders, the federal administration, in particular the departments:

- Federal Department of Defence, Civil Protection and Sport (DDPS)
- Federal Department of Justice and Police (FDJP)
- Federal Department of Foreign Affairs (FDFA)
- Federal Department of Economic Affairs (FDEA).
- Important partners are also the cantons, including 84 national security agents engaged by the Confederation.

Abroad the FIS maintains contacts to more than 100 intelligence, police and security services throughout the world. These bilateral and multilateral contacts have all been authorised by the Federal Council.

Organisation

The FIS's activities and mandate were defined by statute in the Federal Civil Intelligence Act 1997

- the FIS procures security policy relevant information about other countries and evaluates these
- the FIS fulfills intelligence tasks relating to domestic security according to the STA
- the FIS ensures a comprehensive assessment of the threat situation.

And according to the Federal Civil Intelligence Act

- the FIS recognises and combats dangers relating to terrorism, illegal intelligence, violent extremism and proliferation and
- identifies attacks against critical information infrastructure.

The thematic and geographic areas of interest are:

- In Switzerland these are terrorism and violent extremism, proliferation, attacks against critical infrastructure and illegal intelligence activities.
- Abroad, the FIS's thematic areas continue to be proliferation, terrorism, armed forces development, operational areas of our armed forces abroad as well as weapon technology and arms trade.
- The geographic areas of interest continue to be Europe, Russia and the CIS states, the Near East and north Africa, the Middle East, Asia, the USA and hot spots in Africa.

Chapter - 16

Internal Security of Italy

The Ministry of the Interior (Italian: Ministero dell'Interno) is a government agency of Italy, headquartered in Rome.[1] It is cabinet-level ministry of the Italian Republic. As of 1 June 2018, Matteo Salvini is the minister.

The Ministry of the Interior is responsible for internal security and the protection of the constitutional order, for civil protection against disasters and terrorism, for displaced persons and administrative questions. It is host to the Standing Committee of Interior Ministers and also drafts all passport, identity card, firearms, and explosives legislation.

The Ministry of the Interior is political authority for the administration of internal affairs. It controls the State police, the Vigili del Fuoco, and the prefects (it). The minister therefore sits on the High Council of Defence.

The main functions of the ministry are declared in the Executive Order No. 300, promulgated on the 30th of July 1999 and are as follows:

- Ensuring the regular organisation of the elected organs of the local entities and their correct functioning, regulating local finances and electoral services, looking after vital records and registry offices, and collaborating with local entities;
- Protection of public order and security and co-ordination of the police forces;
- General administration and general representation of the government in its territories;
- Protection of civil rights, including religious belief, citizenship, immigration, and asylum.

Currently, the Ministry's duties and powers are regulated by the Presidential decrees of 5 June 1976, no. 676 and 7 September 2001 no.398.

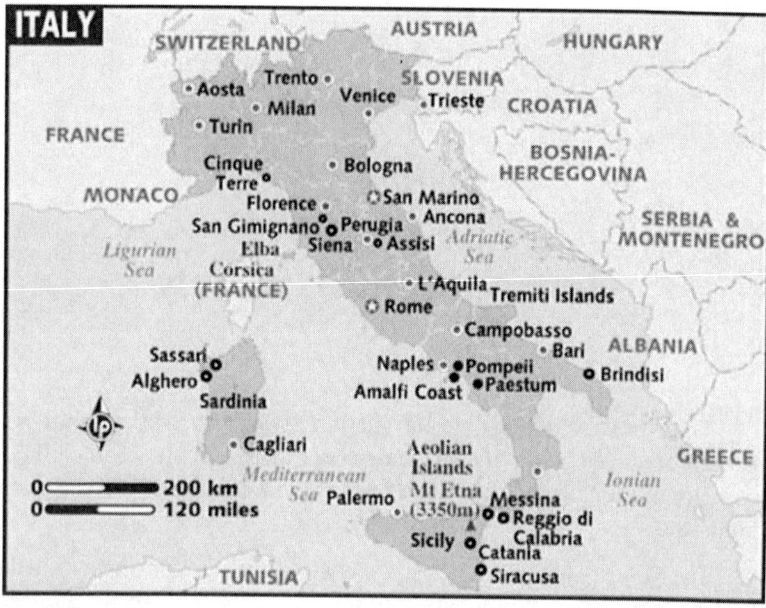

Organisation

The following departments, directorates, special commissions, and other offices and secretariats of the Ministry of Interior are as follows:

Departments

- Department of Public Security (Dipartimento della Pubblica sicurezza)
- Department for Internal and Territorial Affairs (Dipartimento per gli Affari interni e territoriali)
- Department for Civil Liberty and Immigration (Dipartimento per le Libertà civili e l'Immigrazione)
- Department of Firefighters, Public Assistance, and Civil Defence (Dipartimento dei Vigili del fuoco, del Soccorso pubblico e della Difesa civile)
- Department of Civil Administration Policies, Equipment, and Financial Resources (Dipartimento per le Politiche del personale dell'amministrazione civilee perle Risorse strumentali e finanziarie)

Collegial Bodies

- National Committee for Order and Public Safety (Comitato nazionale dell'ordinee della sicurezza pubblica)
- Council of Administration (Consiglio di amministrazione).

Offices for the Direction of Collaboration

- Cabinet of Administration (Gabinetto Ministro)
- Office of Legislative Affairs and Parliamentary Relations (Ufficio
- Independent Organisation for the Valuation of Performance (Organismo indipendente di valutazione della performance)
- Office of the Spokesman for the Ministry (Portavoce del ministro)
- Press and Communications Office (Ufficio stampae comunicazione).

Secretariats

- Secretariat of the Minister of the Interior (Segreteria del ministro)
- Secretariat of the Deputy Minister of the Interior (Segreteria del viceministro)
- Office of the Secretaries of the Secretariat (Segreterie dei sottosegretari).

Special Commissions

- Special Commission for Anti-Racketing and Anti-Usury (Commissario straordinario antiracket e antiusura)
- Special Commission for Missing Persons (Commissario straordinario per le persone scomparse)
- Co-ordinating Commission of Solidarity for Victims of Mafia Crimes (Commissario per il coordinamento delle iniziative di solidarietà per le vittime dei reati di tipo mafioso).

History

The Ministry of the Interior was among the oldest ministries of the Kingdom of Sardinia. It experienced a notable growth in responsibilities from 1861, as a result of the Unification of Italy. As a result of the absence of any kind of Head of Government from the Albertine Statute, the Ministry of the Interior had priority over the Presidency of the Council from the beginning. During the establishment of the unitary state, the Minister of the Interior represented a strongly centralised model of state, desired by the Piedmontese statesmen in order to strengthen the state which they saw as excessively diverse. Along with the Ministry of Finance, the Ministry of the Interior was one of the two pillars on which Italian national unity was built.

The functions of the Ministry were executed by a system of prefectures, based on the French model, with provincial seats whose authority derived from the central government. The attributes of the prefect were intended by the liberal Historical Right government to unify Italy. It was Minister Bettino Ricasoli who initiated this policy of marked centralisation in 1861 with the "Decrees of October." In the first decades of the Kingdom of Italy's existence, the Prefectures gave the government tight control over local affairs, representing the central government locally. In many areas of Italy, the Prefectures were the only offices of the central government.

The Ministry was reorganised in 1870 by Minister Giovanni Lanza and again in 1874 and 1877, under the first government of the left-wing of the Liberal Party. During these years, the Ministry acquired control of the police (separate from the judicial police), prisons, and social policing (meaning offices of public health). Towards the end of the 19th century, Minister Francesco Crispi strengthened the ministry and the prefectures. Subsequently, Minister Antonio di Rudinì decentralised some functions, entrusting various roles to the prefectures which had previously been the responsibility of the Ministry itself.

Under Giovanni Giolitti, in the early twentieth century, the Ministry became the key means of state action. It exercised watchful and strict control over the comuni and provinces, especially in matters of public order. In the arena of public health, it enforced a rationalisation of health laws in 1913, with the so-called "Sanitary Codex". In the social sphere, the prefectures were called upon to mediate in labour conflicts and improve working conditions, in collaboration with the government labour office, and to "municipalise" essential services like tramlines, streetlighting, kindergartens, etc. In this area too, their powers and administrative role expanded.

Although the Ministry continued its ordinary role in maintaining security, order and health during the First World War, its overall structure was not significantly modified. With the rise of Italian Fascism, there was little change. An exception is Law no.1601 of 3 December 1922, which transferred the General Directorate of Prisons and Rehabilitation to the Ministry of Mercy, Justice, and Worship. In general, Benito Mussolini controlled the ministry personally, but it progressively lost its guiding role in the administration of the state.

In 1931, the General Directorate of Support for Worship and of Support for Charity and Religion of the City of Rome, as well as the General Directorate of Religious Affairs, which had previously belonged to the Ministry of Mercy and Justice, were entrusted to the Ministry of the Interior. These offices are still part of the Ministry of the Interior.

After the fall of Fascism, institutional changes resulted from the creation of the Republic of Italy. The main theme of these changes was the increased decentralisation of power to the Regions and the progressive transfer of competencies from the Ministry of the Interior to them over the course of the 1960s.

The main role of the Ministry also changed, or rather reverted to the role it had under Giolitti decades earlier. Its role in social protection was reinforced and, along with the Ministry of Labour it played a key role in welfare politics, providing support to the socially disadvantaged and guaranteeing protection in the event of disaster.

The important sphere of public health was removed from the control of the Ministry in 1958, with the institution of the Ministry of Health. With the creation of the Ministry for Cultural Assets and Environments, the Ministry of the Interior lost control of the Archive of State (it). In the 1980s, the Department of Civil Protection was created, which is headed by an independent Minister without portfolio, but is based on the organisation of the Ministry.

There was also a reorganisation of the centralised structure of the Ministry and the number of General Directorates declined from even to five. Moreover, with Law no. 121/1981, the Polizia di Stato was reformed and transformed from the General Directorate of Public Security into a Department. This anticipated the future departmental structure of the ministry as a whole.

In the 1990s, the Bassanini Reforms (it) involved a complex process of reorganisation of the administrative structure of the Ministry. In particular, Decree Law no.300/1999 dealt with the creation of a departmental structure for the Ministry. Additionally, the prefecture system was overhauled and they were renamed "Government Territorial Prefecture Offices." Since the completion of these reforms, the Ministry has had authority over "general" administration, including relationships between centre and periphery, and particularly for the protection of fundamental functions and the security of citizens.

Headquarters

The Ministry of the Interior has been based in Rome at the Palazzo del Viminale since 1925. Before that, the Ministry, as well as the office of the Prime Minister, were based at the Palazzo Braschi. The Viminale was commissioned in 1911 by Giovanni Giolitti. The architect was Manfredo Manfredi, who was instructed to design a fitting structure for a government headquarters. The Viminale was officially inaugurated on 9 July 1925. The building has five stories and hundreds of rooms linked by a series of hallways. Notable aspects include the imposing triple arched entrance of the Palazzo della Presidenza, the staircase of honour of the Palazzo degli Uffici, the chamber of the Council of Ministers, and entrance to the stairway leading to the piano nobile, with wooden, marble, and stucco decoration.

In 1961, the headquarters of the Office of Prime Minister was separated from the Ministry of the Interior and transferred to Palazzo Chigi, where it remains today.

Chapter - 17

Internal Security of Germany

The German legal system is the product of many centuries of development, starting with the tribal laws of the first Germans. Those indigenous customs were influenced and changed under Roman law and later by the laws that prevailed in the Holy Roman Empire. Feudal law also had a strong influence. When more formal law and legal institutions appeared in the eighteenth century, codes of law and police systems were left to the individual territorial entities. The codes that evolved were mixtures of German, Roman, and ecclesiastical law.

The drive toward political unification during the nineteenth century was accompanied by a trend toward legal unification, especially in commercial matters. In other areas of law, however, the prerogatives of each political entity still governed. Only after the achievement of political unification under Prussian dominance in 1871 was a start made on drawing up German legal codes.

The codes and laws on police and penal institutions adopted after unification showed in varying degrees the influence of the Napoleonic Code. Patterns were established that, despite modifications, continued to prevail. The most important of the early models were the Penal Code of 1871, defining three classes of imprisonment still in use in 1995; the procedural codes of 1877; the law of 1877 establishing a unified court system; and the comprehensive Civil Code, which took effect in its full scope of 2,385 paragraphs in 1900.

Parallel with the courts and laws, there developed a structure of penal institutions and a police system, both characterised by the efficiency for which German administrative organs had long been noted. Although their administration was somewhat relaxed during the Weimar period (1918-33), these bureaucracies tended toward rigidity. The police and penal authorities saw their positions and responsibilities as servants of the state as overshadowing any obligation of service to the people.

When the Nazis came to power in 1933, they capitalised on the tendencies of the legal bureaucracy, centralising control of the police and administration of the courts and making widespread use of special courts. Ostensibly, the laws and institutions remained the same. However, the spirit of the law and the legal system were gradually and totally subverted by the agenda of the Nazi leadership. When the "sound instincts of the people" demanded it, as interpreted by the Nazis, the rule of law was completely ignored.

The impact of Nazi ideology was greatest on the Criminal Code and the Code of Criminal Procedure. The Third Reich greatly broadened the definition of criminal activity, particularly in the category of crimes against the state, and made punishment much harsher. The Code of Criminal Procedure was distorted almost beyond recognition by the activities of the Nazi-inspired People's Court, in which those convicted of crimes against the state were often sentenced to death. In twelve years, an extensive network of special and summary courts of indeterminate jurisdiction was developed.

The police, whose powers and responsibilities were significantly broadened, became tools of the ruling party under the direct control of the minister of interior. The regular police–including city and town forces, motorised gendarmerie in rural areas, and administrative police, who administered codes and regulations–were supplemented by much more powerful internal security units. These included the Security Police (Sicherheitspolizei), which incorporated the Criminal Investigation Police and the Border Police, as well as the newly formed Secret State Police (Geheime Staatspolizei–Gestapo). Two other of Hitler's organisations, the Storm Troops (Sturmabteilung–SA) and the Guard Detachment (Schutz-Staffel–SS), in company with the Gestapo, became infamous as instruments of Nazi brutality.

After World War II, each of the Allied authorities permitted the formation of West German police forces, although under terms that reflected their own police structures and traditions. In all three Western zones, however, the police were decentralised, democratised, and demilitarised. Some restrictions were lifted within two years as Cold War tensions grew, and certain police functions necessitated central rather than local direction. The Federal Border Force was created to handle special functions that overlapped Land jurisdictions. In addition to this force, federal agencies were created to handle inter-state criminal matters and overall security affairs.

The Ministry of the Interior is responsible for internal security and the protection of the constitutional order, for civil protection against disasters and terrorism, for displaced persons, administrative questions, and sports. It is host to the Standing Committee of Interior Ministers and also drafts all passport, identity card, firearms, and explosives legislation. The ministry also houses the Joint Anti-Terrorism Center formed in 2004 which is an information-sharing and analytical forum for all German police and intelligence agencies involved in the fight against terrorism.

Germany's domestic security services explained

Germany's modern security system was founded to prevent the crimes of the Nazi era from ever occurring again. The current system is divided between constitutional protection, criminal police and the regular police.

During the Nazi era, the secret police or Gestapo was granted broad intelligence and security authority. It became something of a state within a state, with citizens left at its mercy. Those who rebuilt Germany after

World War II aimed to distinguish Germany's security agencies from this dark past.

A clear separation of powers, including checks and balances, are built into the security system with this intent. Constitutional protection, criminal police and "regular" police form three separate branches of German security and intelligence-gathering.

Constitutional Protection

The Office for the Protection of the Constitution, founded in 1950, has a very strict mandate: to collect intelligence. Workers are to gather and evaluate "information, news and other documents" that go against Germany's democratic foundations.

This means activities that threaten national or state security, or the "foreign interests" of the country. The office's standard practice is to observe groups or individuals over an extended period of time. Some examples of groups under watch in Germany include the far-right National Democratic Party or NPD, the Turkish-Islamist organisation ICCB and the Church of Scientology.

In contrast to police and the federal prosecutor, the constitutional protection office may investigate when criminal suspicion is lacking. However, it's dependent on the police for any further steps, such as taking people into custody or interrogations. And since domestic security is also a regional matter, the federal office co-ordinates 16 independent state offices.

Method of investigation

The Office for the Protection of the Constitution gets the large part of its information from publicly accessible sources, such as newspapers, flyers programmes and calls to action. Workers visit public events, speaking to people there - and being clearly identified as with the constitutional office. These conversations occur on a "voluntary basis," as the office is not allowed to force anyone to provide information.

Within extremist circles, the office works with so-called connected or trusted people. These are external informants, or private persons who are not undercover agents. Such people could even be "placed" into extreme right-wing groups in order to gain a view into their activities. In this situation, the informants act as if they belong to the group, yet pass along their knowledge to the office. In this capacity, a parliamentary committee can grant them permission to spy on confidential communications. The parliament is involved at this stage because the basic authority for employing informants arises from federal and state law.

Informants may be motivated by several factors, such as to avoid a criminal conviction. Revenge or competition can also play a role. Even financial interest can be a motivating factor, as informants receive a "stipend" for their work from the office.

Criminal Police

The Federal Criminal Police Agency falls under the Interior Ministry, with headquarters in Wiesbaden. Working with state counterparts, this agency co-ordinates the fight against illegal activity. It's also active internationally, with 5,000 staffers among German police partners worldwide. It combats - for example - the weapons and drug trade, counterfeiting, international terrorism, financial crimes and severe cases of computer sabotage. Like the Office for the Protection of the Constitution, it has the ability to employ informants as well.

Police

The job of the German police is to take care of domestic law enforcement - in other words, it seeks to prevent and fight criminality. Under the German constitution, policing is the responsibility of states. Germany's police are therefore distinguished at federal and state levels, with a federal police agency and 16 state police agencies. State police duties and authorities are similar, though not identical across the 16 states. State police are governed by the interior ministry of that state.

Chapter - 18

Internal Security of North Korea

The Ministry of People's Security and the State Security Department are responsible for internal security in North Korea. Although both are government organs, they are tightly controlled by the party apparatus through the Justice and Security Commission and the penetration of their structures by the party apparatus at all levels. The formal public security structure is augmented by a pervasive system of informers throughout the society. Surveillance of citizens, both physical and electronic, is also routine.

People's Security

The Ministry of People's Security, responsible for internal security, social control, and basic police functions, is one of the most powerful organisations in North Korea and controls an estimated 144,000 public security personnel. It maintains law and public order; investigates common criminal cases; manages the prison system and traffic control; monitors citizens' political attitudes; conducts background investigations, census, and civil registrations; controls individual travel; manages the government's classified documents; protects government and party officials; and patrols government buildings and some government and party construction activities.

The ministry has vice ministers for personnel, political affairs, legal counselling, security, surveillance, internal affairs, rear services, and engineering. There are approximately twenty-seven bureaus, but the functional responsibilities of only some of the bureaus are known. The Security Bureau is responsible for ordinary law enforcement and most police functions. The Investigation Bureau handles investigations of criminal and economic crimes. The Protection Bureau is responsible for fire protection, traffic control, public health, and customs. The Registration Bureau issues citizen identification cards and maintains public records on births, deaths, marriages, residence registration, and passports.

Below the ministry level, there are public security bureaus for each province and directly administered city. These bureaus are headed by either a senior colonel or a lieutenant colonel of police, depending on the size of the population. Public security departments at each city or county and smaller substations through the country are staffed by about 100 personnel. They are organised roughly parallel to the ministry itself and have several divisions responsible for carrying out various functions.

State Security Department

In 1973 political security responsibilities were transferred from the Ministry of People's Security to the State Security Department, an autonomous agency reporting directly to Kim Il Sung. The State Security Department carries out a wide range of counterintelligence and internal

security functions normally associated with "secret police" known to North Koreans as Bowibu. It is charged with searching out anti-state criminals—a general category that includes those accused of anti-government and dissident activities, economic crimes, and slander of the political leadership.

Camps for political prisoners are under its jurisdiction. It has counterintelligence responsibilities at home and abroad, and runs overseas intelligence collection operations. It monitors political attitudes and maintains surveillance of returnees. Ministry personnel escort high-ranking officials. The ministry also guards national borders and monitors international entry points. The degree of control it exercises over the Political Security Bureaus of the KPA—which has representatives at all levels of command—is unclear.

The Ministry of People's Security is a law enforcement agency in North Korea. It operates under the umbrella of the State Affairs Commission. Beyond policing, its services include operating the prison system in North Korea, monitoring the public distribution system and providing bodyguards to important persons.

The Ministry of People's Security gathers information from local informers in social units about irregular acts. If a case is believed to be of a political nature, it is instead handed over to the State Security Department for investigation.

The Ministry of Public Security [also termed the Social Safety Ministry] and the State Security Department are responsible for internal security. Although both are government organs, they are tightly controlled by the party apparatus through the Justice and Security Commission and the penetration of their structures by the party apparatus at all levels. The formal public security structure is augmented by a pervasive system of informers throughout the society. Surveillance of citizens, both physical and electronic, also is routine. In 1973 political security responsibilities were transferred from the Ministry of Public Security to the State Security Department, an autonomous agency reporting directly to the President.

The Ministry of People's Security (also known as the Ministry of Public Security) employs roughly 200,000 personnel. Its responsibilities include internal security, social control (such as songbun records and residency restrictions), and basic police functions, including riot suppression.

The Ministry of People's Security is involved in gross violations of human rights. The correctional bureau within the ministry previously operated one of the country's political prison camps (Camp 18) and continues to operate the majority of the country's labor camps (kyohwaso) and other detention/interrogation facilities. Torture and other forms of abuse are reportedly employed regularly as tools of control in these camps.

Defectors have also reported the ministry regularly uses torture and other forms of abuse to extract confessions, including techniques involving sexual violence, hanging individuals from the ceiling for extended periods of time, prolonged periods of exposure, and severe beatings. According to the COI report, almost all of the more than 100 witnesses repatriated from China reported having been "beaten or subjected to worse forms of torture during interrogations" in detention centers run by the ministries of state security and people's security. The COI also reports that inhumane detention conditions also exerted pressure on individuals to quickly confess to secure their survival.

The ministry also enforces the government's censorship policies. According to the COI report, the Communication Maintenance Bureau is responsible for removing the radio components of cassette players (which are legal in the DPRK) to prevent users from listening to foreign broadcasts.

Tight security surrounds Kim Jong Un, even more so than previous North Korean leaders

North Korea is one of the world's most tightly controlled societies, but even so security for its leader is iron clad.

Foreigners attending any event where Kim will be present must go through hours of security procedures beforehand and surrender all electronics, including phones.

The Guard Command, the military unit tasked with ensuring the safety of the leadership, is an elite institution close to the center of North Korean power — it provides the centerpiece display of the annual kimjongilia and kimilsungia flower festivals in Pyongyang to honor Kim's father and grandfather.

Ri Yong Guk, a defector from the North who served on a security detail for Kim Jong Il, wrote in a 2013 memoir that as many as six different layers of security guards protected the leader on trips to the countryside to inspect military units, plants or farms.

"It is one of the world's tightest security blankets through which even a single ant would find it hard to go," he wrote.

The arrangements for the current leader are reportedly even tighter, and during a military parade marking the 70th anniversary of the foundation of its regular armed forces in February, Pyongyang paraded three kinds of security units dedicated to protecting Kim's life.

Kim was repeatedly seen accompanied by a stout military general in uniform with a holstered gun.

The protection afforded to the Kim family was also on display when the leader's sister Kim Yo Jong visited the South for the Pyeongchang Winter Olympics, accompanied by tall bodyguards with crew cuts, sunglasses and earphones.

Former U.S. President Bill Clinton once described the Demilitarised Zone, which divides the peninsula and where Friday's summit was being held, as "the scariest place on Earth."

Despite its name, the DMZ is among the most heavily fortified areas on the planet.

About 50 kilometers (30 miles) north of Seoul, the 4-kilometer-wide space stretches for 250 kilometers across Korea and bristles with electric fences, minefields and anti-tank barriers.

At the joint security area at Panmunjom, the two sides, technically still at war, come face to face, with stern South Korean guards — also chosen for their height and looks — standing stock still only meters from the North Korean positions.

Soldiers are permitted to carry only sidearms in the area, but it is an open secret that both sides have larger weapons stashed nearby for use in case of emergencies.

In November, 2017, a North Korean soldier defected under a hail of automatic rifle fire from Northern troops.

Back in 1984, a 22-years-old Soviet tourist bolted from North to South at Panmunjom, triggering a gun battle in which three pursuing North Korean soldiers were killed, along with a Southern trooper, although defector Vasily Matuzok was unharmed.

Chapter - 19

Donald Trump Met Kim Jong Un

Why was Singapore chosen for Trump-Kim summit? High security

The wealthy city-state of 5.5 million famously fines people thousands of dollars for littering, has banned chewing gum from the streets and still uses caning as a punishment for minor crimes.

Singapore's security is also legendary, which is one major reason it was selected for the historic summit meeting between President Donald Trump and North Korean leader Kim Jong Un, which will be held on Tuesday at the five-star Capella Resort on Sentosa Island.

The country has pulled off other high-stakes meetings in the past, including a 2015 summit between Chinese President Xi Jinping and Taiwan's president at the time, Ma Ying-jeou. Singapore also hosts a major annual defence conference every year that draws political leaders and military brass from around the world.

But the meeting between Trump and Kim is unprecedented, and Singapore is pulling out all the stops to ensure the summit runs smoothly.

North Korea is to be offered unprecedented security guarantees when Kim Jong-un meets Donald Trump in Singapore, the US secretary of state has said on the eve of the summit.

Mike Pompeo did not specify what security assurances Trump would offer Kim but made clear they would go even further than a 2005 agreement in which the US pledged not to attack North Korea with nuclear or conventional weapons.

The White House said Trump would begin his meeting with Kim, the first US summit with North Korea, at 9 pm on Tuesday (2 pm UK time; 9 pm on Monday in Washington) with a one-on-one meeting with translators but no advisers or aides. Only after that initial personal session will national security officials join the meeting.

However, there are doubts over whether Trump can persuade Kim to make a clear statement on his intention to dismantle and surrender his nuclear weapons programme.

If an effort to close the gap, Pompeo said the US could give Pyongyang more guarantees of security than had hitherto been offered.

"It is the case we are prepared to give security assurances necessary for the North Koreans to engage in ... denuclearisation," Pompeo told reporters. "We are prepared to take actions that will provide them sufficient certainty that they can be comfortable that denuclearisation isn't something that ends badly for them."

He added: "We are prepared to make ... security assurances that are different, [more] unique than, what America has been willing to provide previously. We think this is both necessary and appropriate."

US and North Korean officials met in Singapore on Monday to prepare for the historic summit, which will take place at a luxury hotel on an island close to central Singapore.

While North Korea spoke of establishing a new "permanent peace-keeping mechanism" and its state-run news agency hailed a "new era" in relations with the US, Trump tweeted on Monday about how pleased he was to be in Singapore.

Index

T